Broadway Christian Church Fort Way
Different By Design:God's Master Pla... CL.
Burke, H. Dale

P9-DDM-338

0000 7418

DIFFERENT
by DESIGN

DIFFERENT by DESIGN

GOD'S MASTER PLAN FOR HARMONY BETWEEN MEN AND WOMEN IN MARRIAGE

H. DALE BURKE

MOODY PRESS
CHICAGO

© 2000 by
H. DALE BURKE

All rights reserved. No part of this book may be reproduced in any form without permission in writing from the publisher, except in the case of brief quotations embodied in critical articles or reviews.

All Scripture quotations, unless otherwise indicated, are taken from the *New American Standard Bible®*, Copyright © 1960, 1962, 1963, 1968, 1971, 1972, 1973, 1975, 1977, 1995 by The Lockman Foundation. Used by permission.

Scripture quotations marked (NIV) are taken from the *Holy Bible: New International Version®*. NIV®. Copyright © 1973, 1978, 1984 by International Bible Society. Used by permission of Zondervan Publishing House. All rights reserved.

Scripture quotations marked (NKJV) are taken from the *New King James Version*. Copyright © 1979, 1980, 1982 by Thomas Nelson, Inc. Used by permission. All rights reserved.

Scripture quotations marked (NLT) are taken from the *Holy Bible, New Living Translation,* copyright © 1996. Used by permission of Tyndale House Publishers, Inc., Wheaton, Illinois 60189. All rights reserved.

Scripture quotations marked (ASV) are taken from the American Standard Version, © Copyright 1901, Thomas Nelson & Sons; © Copyright 1929, International Council of Religious Education.

Scripture quotations marked (RSV) are taken from the *Revised Standard Version* © 1946, 1952, 1971 by the Division of Christian Education of the National Council of Churches of Christ in the United States of America, and are used by permission. Scripture quotations marked (KJV) are taken from the King James Version.

Library of Congress Cataloging-in-Publication Data

Burke, H. Dale, 1953-
    Different by design / by H. Dale Burke.
        p.cm.
    ISBN 0-8024-8197-3 (pbk.)
    1. Spouses--Religious life. 2. Man-woman relationships--Religious aspects--Christianity. 3. Marriage--Religious aspects--Christianity. I. Title.

BV4596.M3 .B87 2000
248.8'44--dc21

99-086116

1 3 5 7 9 10 8 6 4 2

Printed in the United States of America

To my Lord Jesus Christ,
　　the giver of life,
　　model of grace,
　　and teacher of all truth
　　necessary for any man and woman
　　to enjoy one another and marriage
　　as they walk for a lifetime together.

To my dear wife Becky,
　　my companion for life,
　　model of grace,
　　who has loved me,
　　encouraged and respected me,
　　supported and believed in me,
　　for over twenty-five years.

To the three congregations who believed in me,
supported me, and listened patiently as I taught
God's Word on love and marriage:
　　Oxford Bible Fellowship of Oxford, Ohio
　　Grace Bible Church of Arroyo Grande, California
　　First Evangelical Free Church of Fullerton, California

CONTENTS

FOREWORD

The jagged edges of the man-woman disjunction won't go away. We laugh, we cry, and we swear about them; we try to ignore them and even legislate them into nonexistence. But there they are, girls and boys screeching into society's ears that they are just that—girls and boys—two distinctively different kinds of persons!

Ask God what He meant in His opening scene by the words "God created man in His own image, in the image of God, He created him, male and female He created them" (Genesis 1:27). His reply marches through the pages of the Bible, erecting signposts in every generation. After our first parents' disobedience brought eviction from the Garden of Eden, women apparently lost their voice in civic affairs. Nothing is heard from them except a passing reference to nameless wives and daughters. Cain's great-grandson's two wives are named, a sobering reminder that men had already begun to misuse the privileges of marriage.

Not until the man of faith, Abraham, set out from Haran with his wife, Sarai, is it clear that God has a rescue plan for His daughters as well as His sons. He revealed Himself to the castaway Hagar as El Roi, "the God who sees me." Hebrews 11:11 assures us that Sarah herself was enabled to conceive a son in her old age because she "considered Him faithful who had promised."

Like unearthed gems, the man-woman pairs God used sparkle throughout the pages of the Bible. Jochabed and her husband, Amran; Miriam and her brother Moses, Deborah and Barak; Ruth and Boaz; Hannah and her son Samuel; Mary and Joseph; Priscilla and Aquila; and a host of others testify to God's purpose of heirs together of the grace of God (1 Peter 3:7).

The magnificent splendor of a world balanced by males and females decimates the destructive scheme of Satan to divide and conquer. Made in the image of God, each of the sexes reflects aspects of His likeness. We who are bombarded with distortions of His intended design need more than ever to revise our notions and prejudices about the opposite sex with a refreshment of biblical truth.

Different by Design is a return to reality, the original plan of the Manufacturer. Dale Burke's distinguished pastoral ministry has been marked by significant nourishment of marriages and families. From his pen comes a caring and much-needed word for dwelling in gender harmony.

HOWARD G HENDRICKS
Distinguished Professor and Chairman
Center for Christian Leadership
Dallas Theological Seminary

ACKNOWLEDGMENTS

With special thanks to some special friends, without whom this book would not have been written. I am forever in their debt for the lessons they have taught and the encouragement they have given.

- ❏ Hebron Burke, my late father, and Maxine Burke Marcum, my mother, for modeling faithfulness and leading me to faith.

- ❏ Chuck and Charlotte Melcher, for first teaching me that Jesus is the invisible third partner in my marriage.

- ❏ Howard and Jeanne Hendricks, for giving me a passion for God's Word and its relevance to all of life.

- ❏ Anne Scherich, my editor, whose unseen touch has enriched every page of this manuscript.

Finally . . .

- ❏ My good friend and writer, Jac La Tour, who labored with me to turn rough teaching into polished text. What a joy to partner again with such a gifted wordsmith, who not only hears my words but shares my heart and passion for God-centered relationships.

INTRODUCTION

A really important message, first transmitted at the dawn of creation, has been bouncing around the universe ever since. It's been received by every generation. Some picked up the signal clearly and acted accordingly. For others, it got garbled and they behaved foolishly, or worse.

This is the message: Men and women are worlds apart. Today's generation has proclaimed that men are from Mars and women are from Venus. But are they really all that different? In recent decades, the pendulum has certainly been swinging. As we swung through the 1960s and 1970s, the unisex and feminist movements challenged the idea that gender differences mattered. Sure, there are biological distinctives, but those are merely physical. Under the surface, where it really matters, we were told that men and women are the same. Any behavioral differences are only there because our culture, with its out-of-date, stereotypical notions of masculinity and femininity, has engineered them. Men and women were treated as blank slates, raw material from the womb, ready to be shaped by the culture. The idea that males and females may be different by design was not politically correct. Women were told that it was time to put on the pants and act more like men. Men were to discover their softer side.

In the 1980s and 1990s, the pendulum began to slow down. Movements like Promise Keepers began to call men to be men, but to also be different from men of the past. Women began to again celebrate the value of their unique gifts of nurturing. Some people started to realize that men and women can be equal but at the same time different. It was an important adjustment, a time for us to be reminded that men and women are equally gifted and valued as beautiful, divine creations of our Father in heaven. But in the midst of celebrating all we have in common, we made a critical mistake. We lost sight of our differences and distinctives and the fact that we are different by design. And these differences go much deeper than our reproductive systems or the contours of our bodies. They involve the way we think, feel, and process information and ideas. They involve the way we love and are loved. Most importantly, these differences are healthy. They were designed into us for a reason by our Creator.

This book will not attempt to explain all the mysteries of manhood and womanhood. Rather, our intent is to underscore the fact that God understands all those distinctives, all the subtleties of our nature as men and women. After all, they find their origin in His creative genius. Which means that He always considered our designed-in differences as He issued His directives for building healthy relationships and marriages. By exploring God's Word, we'll discover how to meet the needs of these mysterious beings called men and women.

Why is this mission so important? Because in our culture, differences between men and women often trigger competition between the sexes. Judging from the character of the ancient deities for whom the two nearest planets to Earth are named, ours isn't the only culture to suffer from this competitive tension. Mars, the Roman god of war, borrowed his attributes from the Greek god Ares, who represents "the sudden violence of battle," according to one source. Not only was he often viewed as hostile, but he was also unpredictable, equally likely to help foreigners as Greeks. As for Venus, the Roman goddess of love, she was fickle in her own right, borrowing her attributes from Aphrodite, the Greek's goddess of love. Of course her name is the origin for aphrodisiacs, substances supposedly capable of fueling passion.

There's a subtle irony in the fact that of the more than five hundred aphrodisiacs that have been put forth throughout history as possessing this capacity, none have proved capable of producing anything more than indigestion.

Check out the Bible, though, and you'll quickly see that, while differences between the sexes were part of the original design of the God of the universe, they weren't built in to create friction. Instead, they were intended to complement one another. When they don't, struggles can rock marriage relationships. When those struggles come—and they will come—what we need is some heavenly advice, some down-to-earth biblical guidance, for building healthy marriages.

The good news is that there is help for those who are serious about being better equipped to launch new relationships or make course corrections in relationships that may be straying. That's what this book is all about. Whether you're a newlywed, married with children, or passing advice along to your grandkids, these pages will help you build healthier, stronger relationships by making the *most* of the things we hold *least* in common and appreciating where we are different.

Here's an example. Everyone knows that a spacecraft heats up when it reenters the atmosphere. Relationships between men and women are no different. They can get uncomfortably hot as we enter new ones or new phases of existing ones. The heat comes from friction that's caused by our natural differences. One key for dealing with this natural hazard of navigating marriage is for each person to make it a priority to understand the other's uniquenesses, to value those traits as a source of strength. Common messages in this kind of marriage would be "I respect you" . . . "I need you" . . . "I'm willing to let you be you" . . . "I'll focus on my responsibilities, not my rights."

As we examine the Bible, God's master plan for this mission, we find that the Maker of men and women speaks clearly and with wisdom for the mission. The questions you and I must answer are these: Are we tuned in to mission control or are we trying to fly solo? Are we listening to—or even getting along with—our copilot?

For a smooth flight, it's also essential to jettison any sense of competition based on our differences. A great way is to cultivate a desire to serve. Serving is the great relational equalizer. It replaces unhealthy competitiveness with a genuine message of concern. Jesus set the standard. He "did not come to be served, but to serve" (Mark 10:45), and we should do the same, especially when it involves those we love the most. Again, the Creator's master plan will prove to be our best in-flight resource, providing various instructions with at least one divine illustration for how to have a successful flight by serving our closest crew member.

Naturally, building a healthy marriage requires healthy communication. How do we learn to communicate with someone who seems to be from another planet? Learn that person's language. It won't be easy, and it'll take some time. Part of the hard work is learning how he or she thinks, feels, and responds, and what he or she needs to know. For any marriage to grow strong, openness and honesty need to be the standards. The Scriptures charge us to speak the truth in love (see Ephesians 4:15). This goes double when expressing our hurts, joys, feelings, and dreams. Here again, thankfully, God has not been silent. He has provided an abundance of wise counsel for communication between the sexes. And do we ever need help! For example, the most common complaint among wives—"He doesn't listen!"—is illustration enough that communication is a tough but critically important assignment.

Another law in the universe of relationships is that worlds sometimes collide. When they do, the issue becomes one of how to diffuse the conflict that naturally arises. Jesus was "full of grace and truth" (John 1:14), and so we should desire to excel in these relational essentials. We need to keep the slate clean with the eraser of a forgiving spirit. When dealing with emotional issues, we have to do so truthfully and honestly, but also graciously. A forgiving spirit can heal even the deepest wounds. But what does it mean to forgive? How do you keep from becoming a doormat, from getting bitter? The Bible will show us not only how to grant forgiveness, but also how to receive it. Even what to do when it's being abused.

In the following pages, we will take a journey through Scripture. We'll land on and explore all the major passages on marriage and more. God, the Creator, really does understand His creation. The fact that men and women have much in common as well as dramatic differences is not a surprise to Him. He wired us. He understands us. And best of all, He loves us. He loves us so much that He has not left us alone like space travelers without a star map, because He knows that the universe of relationships, especially between the sexes, can be a tricky one to navigate. Whether you presently feel lost and wounded or on course and healthy, or are just beginning the journey, His words are for you.

Maybe it's time for you to do a serious diagnostic check on your marriage. Maybe your mission is already in trouble. If you need to bring Mars and Venus down to Earth, you've come to the right book. Because the best advice is not found on talk shows or call-in radio programs. You can only find it in the Book, the Bible. And that's where we're headed. So sit back, strap yourself in, and join us as we seek out heavenly advice and boldly go where God has gone before.

CHAPTER ONE

OFF TO A (SOMEWHAT) HEAVENLY START

When God launches a mission, one thing's for certain. He'll get where He's going every time, right? Hey, He's God. Maker of Mars and Venus and the whole rest of the universe. Let's say His mission is to create something—planets, people, new life, new civilizations, whatever. The result will always be the same. When the mission is over, and He pulls back to size up His work, He *will* be a satisfied Creator. It's all going to be there, everything in working order, no missing parts. Everything.

Everything? Why don't we check the master plan and find out?

The Bible is the log of God's eternal mission, and the Creation account is His first entry. Captain's log, Genesis, chapter 1. Five brief paragraphs record the events. Leave it to the Maker of heaven and earth to reduce the creation of the universe to so few words. Like any log, the events are recorded with utmost efficiency, which means any words that are repeated immediately attract your attention. As you read these five entries, notice the evaluation at the end of each day:

> God called the dry land earth, and the gathering of the waters He called seas; and God saw that *it was good.* (Genesis 1:10, emphasis added)

*The earth brought forth vegetation, plants yielding seed after their kind, and trees bearing fruit with seed in them, after their kind; and God saw that **it was good**.* (Genesis 1:12, emphasis added)

*God made the two great lights . . . to govern the day, and . . . the night. . . . And God saw that **it was good**.* (Genesis 1:16, 18, emphasis added)

*God created the great sea monsters and every living creature that moves . . . and every winged bird after its kind; and God saw that **it was good**.* (Genesis 1:21, emphasis added)

*God made the beasts of the earth after their kind, and the cattle after their kind, and everything that creeps on the ground after its kind; and God saw that **it was good**.* (Genesis 1:25, emphasis added)

So far, so good. The creation mission was off to a great start. All systems go. But then something changed. The Scripture log rewinds and zooms in on the action, giving us something like an instant replay. To this point, *it was good* at the end of each day's work. Five times those words were repeated. But now we read:

*Then the Lord God said, "**It is not good** for the man to be alone."* (Genesis 2:18, emphasis added)

Come again? This sounds strangely similar to, "Houston, we have a problem." But wasn't this God's mission? Yes, it was. And for the first time the Creator was dissatisfied with His work. Something was missing. By this time God had made Mars and Venus . . . and Adam, the first male, but it became quickly apparent that it was "not good for man to be alone." Naturally, God had a solution.

The Lord God fashioned into a woman the rib which He had taken from the man, and brought her to the man. The man said,

> *"This is now bone of my bones,*
> *And flesh of my flesh;*
> *She shall be called Woman,*
> *Because she was taken out of Man."*
> —Genesis 2:22–23

When Adam first laid eyes on Eve, a rough paraphrase of his sentiments might be, "Wow! Look at this creature! She's incredible! Lions and tigers and bears . . . oh my, they're OK, but she's something special. She's . . . like me. Then again, she's different too. Wow!" OK, maybe this is a stretch, but Adam definitely liked what he saw. And his thumbs-up response leads to the final conclusion:

*God saw all that He had made, and behold, it was **very** good.* (Genesis 1:31, emphasis added)

Even with the momentary glitch, it was a great beginning. Man and woman were now both on the scene, inhabitants of planet Earth. They may not have come from Mars and Venus, but their arrival was no less spectacular. And from the Creator's log, we can make two important observations. The first is this:

Men and women are the same,
***equally honored* by God.**

This equality shows up in three areas.

Men and women are equally honored in creation. This is how Genesis records it: "God created man in His own image, in the image of God He created him; male and female He created them" (1:27). There is no hint here that women are anything but equal to men. Eve was nothing like all those lions and tigers and bears, oh my, not to mention the thousands of other animals Adam had just spent so much time naming. Not even close. To his credit, he saw right off that, like him, she was unique in all creation. She alone shared with him the distinction of being created in God's image. She obviously shared God's blessing as well, and Adam picked up on this blessing. When he said that she was "bone of my bones, and flesh of my flesh" (Genesis 2:23), he was elevating and praising Eve for who she alone was—his equal in the eyes of their Maker.

It's important to notice here that there is no hint of female inferiority in the Creation account. Eve was made of the same stuff as Adam. The right stuff. They were *both* unique among all of God's creation, made in the very image of God Himself. They were spirit beings with eternal souls who were designed to relate in a beautiful way to the eternal God of creation.

Notice too that the primary focus wasn't then, and isn't today, one of physical appearance. God is spirit, not flesh, as Jesus declared:

*God is **spirit**, and those who worship Him must worship in **spirit** and truth.* (John 4:24, emphasis added)

The apostle Paul concurred:

*The **Spirit** Himself testifies with our **spirit** that we are children of God.* (Romans 8:16, emphasis added)

The point is, men and women are absolutely in a category of their own on planet Earth and throughout the universe. They are, from Creation, born with a calling to relate, to know and love their Creator, and to reflect His image.

Yes, we have sinned and are fallen and that image is therefore marred. But we are still the pinnacle of God's creation: Eve at the side of Adam, man and woman, both as eternal spiritual beings who bear the image of God. The implications of this fact on how we treat one another will be explored throughout this book. For now, though, just log this truth away: Men and women are equal in creation.

This notion should strike citizens of the United States of America as, well, self-evident, just as it did those who founded this nation. Listen to the opening words of our own Declaration of Independence.

When in the Course of human events, it becomes necessary for one people to dissolve the political bands which have connected them with another, and to assume among the powers of the earth, the separate and equal station to which the Laws of Nature and of Nature's God entitle them, a decent respect to the opinions of mankind requires that they should declare the causes which impel them to the separation.

We hold these truths to be self-evident, that all men are created equal, that they are endowed by their Creator with certain unalienable Rights, that among these are Life, Liberty and the pursuit of Happiness.

Do you get the picture? As the Founding Fathers recognized, we're all "created equal."

Men and women are equally honored in Christ. If you jump to the New Testament, you'll find these words from the apostle Paul:

> *For all of you who were baptized into Christ have clothed your-selves with Christ. There is neither Jew nor Greek, there is neither slave nor free man, there is neither male nor female; for you are all one in Christ Jesus.* (Galatians 3:27–28)

Paul's words are crystal. Like God the Father, as far as Christ is concerned, men and women are equal. No, this doesn't mean that at times in the life of the church, for example, or in the home, male and female roles won't be different. (We'll talk more about this later on.) Paul wasn't talking about assuming the same roles; he was talking about assuming the same identity. Male or female, we are Christians—both highly valued, divinely chosen, significantly gifted children of the King! When it comes to gender, there are no second-class citizens in the kingdom.

One common error in the logic of our culture is the assumption that role distinctions among men and women must imply inequality. Don't buy it. Different roles on a team do not mean that teammates are unequal. To say that would be as absurd as suggesting that the man on a mixed-doubles tennis team is more important than the woman. As on the tennis court, the roles or re-sponsibilities God calls us to as men and women are often the same. In fact, the vast majority of God's plan for us is directed to all, both men and women. As children of God, we are assured that He values both daughter and son alike. The fact, which we will study later, that God also has a *unique calling* for men as husbands and women as wives should never call into question the core val-ue of men or women in Christ. In the Savior, as His children, we are one, equally gifted and valued. In both creation and in Christ, men and women are equal—but there's more.

Men and women are equally honored with the riches of God's grace. Peter put it like this when addressing husbands: "And show her [your wife] honor as a fellow heir of the grace of life" (1 Peter 3:7).

We need to recognize what a radical cultural shift this view represented for Peter, Paul, and the other apostles. To say that women shared in the riches that we inherit meant that women were equally gifted, equally honored, equally prepared to live for God and walk with Him. To understand how at odds this view was with the culture, look at these words of Aristotle, one of the great influences on Greek thinkers of that day.

> A female is a deformed male. The male seed, implanted in the female, will produce male offspring unless the seed is defective or affected negatively by an external influence such as a south wind which is moist.

Talk about gender issues. All it takes, according to the prevailing wisdom of the ancient Greek world, is a moist south wind and you're in trouble. Not a very esteeming view of women, was it? But the Greeks weren't alone. In that day there was also a common Jewish daily prayer that said, "I thank my Lord that I am not a Gentile nor a woman." This is the culture out of which Paul came and to which he wrote, "[In Christ] there is neither male nor female" (Galatians 3:28). It is to this culture that Paul said, "You [Christians] are all one in Christ Jesus" (Galatians 3:28), and to which Peter said, "You [Christian] husbands" show your wives "honor as a fellow heir of the grace of life" (1 Peter 3:7).

Our differences are obvious, but when it comes to our standing before God, women and men are the same, equally honored by Him. It's important that we get this straight if we're going to build healthy relationships. How important?

This is ground zero. This is where healthy relationships are launched. Unfortunately, the pendulum has swung too far in both directions over the years. For centuries, feminine traits were denigrated and women were underappreciated and often oppressed. Women were often treated as second-class citizens of God's kingdom. They were relegated to rolling bandages for the missionaries, running the nursery, or keeping those potlucks hot and tasty. In the home, they were to fulfill their support role faithfully while being careful to stay in their places. Husbands seldom consulted with their wives, leading their families as if the wives were simply silent, live-in servants.

I do not mean to imply that all churches operated this way, but far too often this was the case. Women truly were viewed and therefore treated as inferior to men. Masculinity was strong and esteemed. Femininity was weak and devalued. For this abuse of

God's Word and the women and wives of His kingdom we as men must say "We're sorry." We must value women as the gifts and strengths of God's creation that they are. But as is often true, in its zealous attempt at a course correction, our culture has driven us too far off course in the other direction. A brutal bumper sticker I saw the other day underscores how far this shift has taken us. It read: "Women who want to be equal to men lack ambition."

In today's world, it is now fashionable to bash both men and many things we call masculine. A quick review of sitcoms displays a long line of males portrayed as insensitive, immature misfits who are emotional and marital cripples. From the Archie Bunkers of an earlier generation to Bart Simpson today, the message of the media too often is that men are miserable excuses for partners in this grand adventure called marriage.

Perhaps the worst example appeared in an otherwise hilarious and popular program that topped the ratings for the better part of its ten-year run on prime-time television. I'm talking about the character George Costanza in the sitcom *Seinfeld*. Frankly, none of the guys on the show, including the star, could have won awards for sensitivity to women. But there was one guy who thought of nothing but women and whose every thought of them or word to them was either selfish or demeaning or downright demented. The sad part is that, like most good comedy, this character's weird ways with women were funny because there was just enough truth in them.

Somewhere between these extremes is where we find the truth, that God has created men and women as different, but no less equal. Masculinity and femininity are both good, both valuable and equally essential for healthy friendships or families. If God thought we needed a world of just men, He would have provided Adam with an Eddie, not an Eve. If He only valued a feminine touch, He could have created Adam with a strictly softer, sensitive side. The truth is, though, that the beauty and diversity of our Creator is best displayed in Adam and Eve as a team. The best of all we call feminine—tenderness, gentleness, mercy—flows from the image of God. Likewise, those qualities deemed more masculine—toughness, strength, courage—spring from our God who represents all of these.

I am not implying that men don't need to nurture that softer side. Nor would I suggest that women cannot nor should not display strength, toughness, or fortitude. God calls both men and women, husbands and wives, to be tough and tender, people of justice and mercy, "full of grace and truth" as we imitate Jesus. But most would agree the evidence is undeniable that as male and female we start from different points. And my point, which I believe is God's point, is that that's OK. It's just the way He planned it.

But this is only half the story. The next point is that the Bible also makes something else clear, which is our second major observation:

Men and women are *different,*
uniquely and wonderfully fashioned by God.

This begins to come clear when God said, "It is not good for the man to be alone; I will make him a helper suitable for him" (Genesis 2:18).

A helper suitable for him. To get the picture here, you need to understand two words. The Hebrew word for "helper" means to be a support, one who comes alongside to encourage and assist you, to complete you. It obviously refers to someone who is different. Down through history, this text has often been wrongly used to teach that women, the helpers, are inferior to men, that their role is one of subservience. This view misses the mark by more than a few light-years. This same word is used nineteen times in other Genesis passages; sixteen times it refers to how God, or Yahweh, is the helper of Israel . . . the helper for us. Do you see the significance? This term is used to describe God! There's no way it implies inferiority. The helper is different, yes. Distinctly different. But as we learned earlier, no less equal.

The helper completes, assists, fills in the gaps. God did just that for Israel and continues to be a "helper" to us today. Dare I imply that as my "help in time of need" (Hebrews 4:16) He is inferior to me? No way! However, for God to truly help me, He must be different from me. It's the same for my wife. Just as a puzzle is not made up of identical pieces, neither is a marriage, which is the emphasis of the second key word.

That word is the term *suitable,* and it is a particularly interesting word. It's from a Hebrew word most commonly translated "in front of." It's also translated sixteen times in the Old

Testament as "opposite." God was saying, "I will make you a helper opposite you, or in front of you." I think the essence of what He was saying is, "I want to make one who will complement you, but this person is not going to be exactly like you." The last thing any of us needs is someone exactly like us.

A suitable helper. One who will complement another. One who will complete the other. God is talking about women being similar to but different from men for good reason. How different? Just stop by a local park during baseball season and you'll find out.

I'm talking about the difference between a guys' little league game and a girls' softball game. To the casual observer, baseball and softball are pretty much alike. Pitch. Hit. Catch. Throw. But the similarities end right there. I realized this a couple of years ago as I watched our son's little league games and our daughter's softball games. Let's say the girls are up to bat first. Here's the typical routine:

Coach gathers the team in a circle and they all join hands.
Everybody (enthusiastically and often with a touch of choreography): "With a B-B-B and an A-A-A and an L-L-L, hit the ball!"
The circle breaks and they all pile into the dugout as if they're boarding a bus for Disneyland.

If the guys bat first, things start differently:

Coach (gruffly): "OK, everybody in here!"
The players bunch up in a circle and stick their hands in the middle.
Coach: "One. Two. Three . . ."
Players (in monotone unison): "Hunh!" (This is guy talk for: "With a B-B-B and an A-A-A and an L-L-L, hit the ball!")
The guys walk quietly, in manly fashion, to the dugout, sit down, put on their game faces, and spit every once in a while.

Throughout their respective games, the differences between boys and girls are glaring. On the field, the guys are all business, grunting occasional one-liner baseball clichés like "Hey, batter, batter, batter" or "Hum babe, fire hard" (guy talk for "Throw a

27

fastball"). Of course they're having fun, but it's not cool to show it. When the game's over there are the mumbled obligatory chants for the winners and a few tough-guy high fives all around—and then the players head to the car. The losers have it written all over their faces.

Meanwhile, over on the softball diamond, a carnival atmosphere prevails. On the field, the girls are singing. Smiling. Laughing. Obviously having fun. In the dugout, every player not batting is busy cheering. Hit, walk, or strikeout, no matter. The bench is on your side. In fact, they get everybody on your side. While the guys sit stoically when they're in the dugout, the girls all hop on the bench, spin around to face the crowd, and lead a cheer (all accompanied by a well-rehearsed dance routine in the dugout): "Stand up! Clap your hands! Get some spirit in the stands!"

After the game, it's join hands time again around the pitcher's mound for the winners to give their opponents another specially choreographed cheer, then rush over to their dugout and form a human tunnel for them to run through, cheering all the way. During postgame snack time, don't bother asking who won the game. They're just all glad to be together. One big happy team. For them, it's not about winning or losing. It's about relating.

Same game. But depending on who's playing, it's a *very* different game. Why? Because of the way God made them.

In an earlier day, women may have been criticized for not being competitive enough, for lacking that killer instinct to put away the enemy (make that "opponent"), and today, our girls are getting tougher. Now the boys are viewed as inferior because they lack sensitivity. So society continues to try and make its men more tender and its women tougher. Is this a bad idea? Of course not. God wants men and women, boys and girls to mature toward Christlikeness, toward godliness. But let's not forget that these differences are also part of God's original design so that we can compete in *life,* not with one another. It's not male versus female, but together, as a team it's male *and* female versus life.

So what have we learned? Here are three tips to get us started as a team. Think of them as a review of all we've said so far. Accept, appreciate, and think team.

1. Men and women were different from day one, so *accept their differences.* There's been a tendency in our culture to view

some of the attributes of women as inferior. Feminine attributes like nurturing or deep caring or emotional sensitivity have sometimes been portrayed as weaknesses. That is not the biblical view. Then again, as the pendulum has swung the other way in recent years, it's become politically correct for women to bash males and ridicule their masculinity. Actually, the pendulum started swinging as far back as the 1970s. What was that fill-in-the-blank line Gloria Steinem came up with? "A woman without a man is like a fish without _____." Her answer: a bicycle. It's funny, but it's out of balance too. God's Word says our differences are intentional, and we should both accept them.

After Becky and I were married, we had to face the fact that we handle conflict differently. I'm a quick closer. I hate unresolved tension. When I know I've blown it, I'm eager to confess, kiss, and make up—now! Becky agrees with one-third of my approach. She's eager for me to confess, but the kissing and making up parts come a little slower for her. She needs time to process the hurt I've caused. She needs cooldown time. I'm like the gas jets on a stovetop. When you turn them off, they're off. Becky's more like an electric range. She can turn off the juice to the burner, but it stays hot to the touch for a while. So I need to give her some time to cool off. And that's OK. We both need to deal with it quickly, but how quickly can vary from one person to another.

2. Men and women are uniquely designed by God, so *appreciate them.* God is the One who thought these two creatures up, men and women. God designed them, differences and all, and it's normal to appreciate, even be attracted by, these differences. I like the way one researcher put it. After surveying nearly twenty-five thousand couples, this is what he discovered:

> The strange and beautiful Venusians were a mysterious attraction to the Martians. Their differences especially attracted the Martians. Where the Martians were hard, the Venusians were soft. Where the Martians were angular, the Venusians were round. Where the Martians were cool, the Venusians were warm. In a magical and perfect way their differences seemed to complement each other.[1]

That's reality. Appreciate the differences.

To make this insight really practical, I'd suggest that you make a list of the top five differences between yourself and your wife or husband. Begin to pray and thank God for those differences. Ask Him to help you see how they add strength to the fabric of your marriage.

To get a picture of how these complementary differences can create strength, take a close look at a piece of plywood. You'll see that that remarkably sturdy sheet of building material is comprised of surprisingly flimsy layers of wood. But when those layers are glued together at perpendicular angles, the resulting product is so strong that it was used in the construction of the first airplanes and is a mainstay of the construction industry today. Note, too, how plywood's strength in turn brings resilience to whatever it is used to construct. Similarly, a strong relationship can be a source of stability to those who are associated with it.

So, instead of sweating the differences, talk about the advantages of being different. Some of the very qualities that cause you friction can become reasons to celebrate.

3. Finally, men and women are designed to support each other, so *think team!* God wants us to work together, to use our differences to make us both stronger. The best teams are always built on common goals and values, yet different skills and strengths are needed to balance each other out. It's interesting that most couples are attracted, initially, to areas of common interest. But then real love, especially romantic love, is often cemented by an appreciation of our differences.

A number of years ago, I met a couple who illustrated this perfectly. I'll call them Jack and Jill. They were college students attending my church. They were the ideal couple. Both were involved in the same Christian organization. They had the same values. Similar life goals drew them together. They fell in love, were soon married after some premarital counseling by yours truly, and their marriage got off to a great start. But it wasn't long before increasing friction began to heat up their relationship. In no time, they went from being madly in love to being just . . . mad.

Jill was especially mad as, on the brink of divorce, they came to talk with me. I remember asking her, "What was it, Jill, that drew you to Jack?"

"You know what attracted me to Jack?" she asked in reply. "I always admired his temperament. He was steady and solid. Nothing ever rattled him. And when I blew it, like I did a lot with my quick temper, he wouldn't react to my anger. He kept his cool and forgave me."

"Well then, what's the problem?" I probed.

"The problem is I'm trying to get us to deal with our issues," she said, "but he won't get off his duff. He's so blasted steady and solid it's like he's planted in cement! And if I get mad and yell at him, it doesn't do any good. Do you know what he does? He forgives me!"

She was serious. The very things that had attracted her to Jack were repulsive now that she lived with him every day.

The mission men and women face every day is not only how to live with our differences but, once we get into relationships, to figure out how to turn them into strengths. We really seem to be from different worlds. So did God make a "mistake" by creating us so different? I don't think so. Remember, He said it was very good. You see, God had a plan for bringing these two worlds together. The two really can become one.

But how? As we're about to discover, no relationship is a better proving ground for this all-important assignment than marriage.

NOTE

1. John Gray, *Men Are from Mars, Women Are from Venus* (New York: Harper Collins, 1992), 44.

CHAPTER TWO

SEVEN GIFTS THAT BRING OUR WORLDS TOGETHER

Anyone who doesn't think God has a sense of humor hasn't paid enough attention to the Creation account. Think about it. First He created all the animals, then He made a most unique creature—Adam—to rule over all the others. Now, to enable Adam to fulfill that role effectively, God gave him an assignment . . . to name all the animals. And if I'm getting the gist of the text in Genesis 2, God paraded those beasts past His prototype human being in pairs. Check out the biblical account.

> Then the Lord God said, "It is not good for the man to be alone; I will make him a helper suitable for him." Out of the ground the Lord God formed every beast of the field and every bird of the sky, and brought them to the man to see what he would call them; and whatever the man called a living creature, that was its name. The man gave names to all the cattle, and to the birds of the sky, and to every beast of the field, but for Adam there was not found a helper suitable for him. (Genesis 2:18–20)

Do you see the humor? Here's Adam, all by his lonesome, giving names to all these creatures who, it would appear from the text, are . . . unalone. Why get Adam involved in this exercise?

Was it that God couldn't come up with enough names for so many animals? Or could it be His clever way of saying, "Hey, Adam. Do you see all these creatures parading past you in pairs? One tiger, one tigress. One buck, one doe. One he bear, one she bear. Where is your pair, Bud? This is not rocket science, my man. *There's only one of you!*" Apparently it was taking Adam too long to figure it out, because the text suggests his Maker was the One who pointed out the obvious: "For Adam there was not found a helper suitable for him." The solution was, well, divine.

So the Lord God caused a deep sleep to fall upon the man, and he slept; then He took one of his ribs and closed up the flesh at that place. The Lord God fashioned into a woman the rib which He had taken from the man, and brought her to the man. (Genesis 2:21–22)

Another thing I find delightfully funny is to think about that moment when Adam woke up and saw God's solution to the missing component in his life. Think about it. What must have run through Adam's groggy mind when he opened his eyes? As far as we know, there was no presurgery briefing. No blueprints, sketches, or "artist's rendering" to be reviewed ahead of time. God had His design and He wasn't about to let Adam mess with it.

After He administered some divine anesthesia to put Adam to sleep, He was careful to leave no doubt that Eve was Adam's partner, his complement—He took a rib from Adam's side. If ever there was a question as to the value of women in God's eyes, remember that while Adam came from dirt, Eve came from the flesh of God's prized possession. And so God finished His masterpiece. The perfect wife and mother of the human race! There she stood, magnificent, beautiful, but just a little (dare I say it?) different.

I gained a whole new appreciation for Adam's experience after I ruptured my Achilles tendon a few years ago. Just like Adam, I went under general anesthesia for the surgery, and just like Adam, I was greeted by a beautiful woman when I regained consciousness. It was my wife Becky standing at my bedside. At that moment, I acquired a much deeper appreciation for Adam's response: "This is now bone of my bones and flesh of my flesh." Seems like there should be an exclamation point at the end of that statement, doesn't it? If that had been you or me, I could see us saying something like, "Wow, look at this creature, this beautiful creation that

You have made, God. She's just like me. But . . . she's different too. And wow, what a difference! Talk about new and improved. And what's even more amazing is that she's *from* me! We are one. I'm telling You, I like her. A lot!"

Did you realize that we've just reviewed the account of when God established marriage? This is the story of how He created the first couple. And embedded in it, I believe, is God's wisdom for having a healthy marriage. Look at it this way. If God were doing your premarital counseling, what would He say to you about marriage? Let's look more closely at these verses and see if we can't get a clearer picture of what marriage can be when two people who are designed differently come together God's way.

I call these insights "God's Great Marriage Seven." As we consider each one, we'll look at three components—the *need* that's identified, then the *role* you must play, and then the *gift* you can give to meet that need. You see, as men and women, male and female, we have needs that cry out to be met in and through this new relationship. In this great Creation epic, we can see the very first indications—some subtle, some obvious—of at least seven *needs* that are met in marriage: companionship, help, balance, esteem, security, intimacy, and acceptance.

Each of these seven needs challenges us as spouses to assume seven matching roles. To the degree to which we learn to play these *roles,* not as actors and actresses but genuinely, from the heart, we serve one another and in the process fulfill the seven needs. These roles are: friend, assistant, completer, fan, loyal lover, romantic lover, and listening lover.

THE MARRIAGE SEVEN
GENESIS 2:18–25

The Need	Your Role	The Gift
Companionship	Friend	Time
Help	Assistant	Servant-Spirit
Balance	Completer	Perspective
Esteem	Fan	Praise
Security	Loyal Lover	Commitment
Intimacy	Romantic Lover	Sexual Love
Acceptance	Listening Lover	Unconditional Love

To meet these needs, however, and to play these roles, we must be givers and takers. Each role requires a different *gift,* and these gifts hold the secrets to a loving, vibrant marriage. The seven gifts are: time, servant-spirit, perspective, praise, commitment, sexual love, and unconditional love. Before we examine each of these needs, roles, and gifts in more detail, look at the diagram on page 35 to help you see each one and where they all come from.

Let's look at each one of these areas in more detail.

WE NEED COMPANIONSHIP

It is not good for the man to be alone. (Genesis 2:18a)

The need. Marriage is designed to solve the problem "It is not good for man, or woman, to be alone." When God said, "I will make him a helper suitable for him," He was addressing a fundamental need of every man and woman—the need for *companionship.* All of us, male and female, share this need. With relationships strained at every turn, we need to know that someone will be there for us when life's load seems too much to bear alone. And when things are going great, we need someone to celebrate with us. Whether weeping or rejoicing, we need someone to share in the experience. Interestingly, meeting this need is one of the goals of marriage. In Genesis, it was Adam who needed companionship, but listen to what a researcher came up with after interviewing thousands of women on this subject.

> Most men have little awareness of how important it is to a woman to feel supported by someone who cares. Women are happy when they believe their needs will be met. When a woman is upset, overwhelmed, confused, exhausted, or hopeless what she needs *most* is *simple companionship.*[1]

Isn't that interesting? This researcher concluded the same thing that's found in God's Word. This insight isn't new—it's multiple millennia old. But it's still true. We all need companionship, for someone just to be there. So often, as a pastor, I encounter people in grief. I've never been good with words at times like that, but I learned years ago that mere presence, though silent, conveys the all-important message "I care." It's no different with our spouses. Guys often think that their wives want them to do something, but often the most important response is simply being there.

Your role. It was a wise person who observed that a *friend* is one who walks in when the rest of the world is walking out. The lesson from this adage is clear: It's in the role of a friend that we're best able to meet another's need for companionship. If you're serious about appreciating the differences between you and your mate, be there when he or she needs you. Be a friend. And remember, as Joanna Baillie (1762–1851) reminds us, building friendship is a long labor.

> Friendship is no plant of hasty growth;
>
> Tho' planted in esteem's deep, fixed soil,
>
> The gradual culture of kind intercourse
>
> Must bring it to perfection.

The gift. What gift can we give to most effectively meet this need? It's simple, but of enormous value. It's the gift of *time*. When you make time to be with your companion, you're saying "I love you" in the most emphatic way possible. The fact that sometimes simply being with my wife is what she needs most is almost too much for my masculine mind to grasp. And I know I'm not the only guy to whom sitting quietly with my wife "doing nothing" can seem like a waste of time when my to-do list is a mile long. But whenever I make time to be with Becky, to give her the gift of time, I'm reminded that the quietness of that setting whispers a reassuring message to my wife: "I love you. I care. I'm here for you. I'm available."

One of the best moves we ever made was to set aside Mondays, my day off, as our day. A pastor's life can be busy, even hectic. So, more than twenty-five years ago, we dedicated this day to just being together. The temptation to go our own way and pursue our own agendas is real, so we do just about everything together on Mondays. And even though it's less efficient to tackle the day's tasks or projects together, we've found it to be an investment that pays big dividends in our marriage.

As you plan activities, though, remember that you are different by design. Here are a few ways to be together that we've found to be fun and inexpensive yet which meet both our needs. Come up with your own list and add to it regularly.

- A bike ride . . . with a midpoint milk shake break
- A shopping trip . . . with a list for me to shop for
- Read a book . . . and talk about what we both like and dislike about it
- Go to a park or the beach . . . and take a nap
- Swing by a nice restaurant for dessert and coffee . . . after the rush hour

WE NEED HELP

I will make him a helper suitable for him. (Genesis 2:18)

The need. When two different people come together in marriage, life switches from an individual sport to a team effort. And the very nature of teams is that the individual members need *help* from the others if they hope to succeed. Whether it's water polo or rugby, soccer or basketball, the team's success depends on each member helping the others. Mounting a team effort, though, can become tougher as life's demands pull us in opposite directions. This is particularly true as families grow. Each new family member increases the number of communication contacts in the home dramatically. A couple has just one communication line between them. Add a child and the number triples—wife to husband, wife to child, and husband to child. A second child increases the number to six, a third takes it to ten, and a fourth child boosts the total all the way to fifteen lines of communication in the home. And let's face it, maintaining that number of relationships can not only make for a busy life; it can elevate the need for help from *optional* to *essential.* As the family team expands, the need to work together as husband and wife cannot be ignored.

A couple in our church perfectly illustrates this reality. Kaya and Dave Lien have seven children, all of whom are now college age and older. But when the kids were still at home, Kaya and Dave found that teamwork was the only way to manage their household and keep their marriage strong. At one point, Kaya worked out an age-appropriate system of dividing up household responsibilities among the kids that accounted for other essentials like homework. Their system provided enough structure that Kaya and

Dave weren't run ragged trying to stay on top of all the chores as they nurtured their relationships with their kids and each other. When I asked Dave about those hectic days of their family life, he was quick to say that the bulk of the help came from Kaya, and that it wasn't just him she sought to help.

"Actually, I was the one who needed the structure back then," he said. "Kaya was the key to what we did, though. She was a servant who had the kids' interests in mind all the time. And she was *always* communicating with them. At home, driving in the car, wherever, she engaged their interests. That was crucial. And one more thing. Back then we drew a lot of hard lines in our family and in our marriage. Now, thirty-six years into our relationship, we don't have many hard lines anymore. What we do have is a lot of dialogue."

Regardless of our family's size, we should follow Kaya and Dave's example. Help one another. And if we're going to draw lines, make them communication lines.

Your role. If you look on the sidelines of any team sporting event, certain people are easy to spot. The head coaches usually catch your attention because they're the most nervous. Often they're also quiet or reflective, planning the next move for the team. Few, if any players, are talking to them. Beside and behind every head coach, though, you'll find at least one *assistant* scurrying up and down the sideline or along the bench handling details, giving directions, taping ankles, passing water to the players. Which is most important? Fact is, they could never succeed without one another. The same holds true in many professions. Backing up one person you'll often find another, someone who is there to help whenever and wherever they're needed. In marriage, when one partner needs help, the other assumes that all-important role of assistant.

To get a picture of how crucial this role is, you need look no further than a basketball or hockey game. One of the key statistics in each of these sports is "assists." A player earns one every time he or she passes the ball or puck to someone else who scores. The implication is beautifully obvious. The team that gets the most assists gets the most points and comes out the winner. So it is in marriage. Take the role of assisting your mate seriously and you'll both come out winners.

The gift. Now, in your role as an assistant, you're going to have to make a decision, and this is it: Will you be a willing worker or a resentful one? My experience is that having no help at all is better than having an assistant with an attitude. So what's the best gift you can give to meet this need? I say the gift of help with a *servant-spirit*. If you're a husband, the admonition in Ephesians 5 is to nourish your wife (see v. 29). And Philippians 2 says that we're to serve one another in love (see also Galatians 5:13). So, whatever planet you're from, when your worlds come together, decide on the front end that you're going to bring a servant-spirit to the relationship. (Chapter 3 will explore Philippians 2 and the role of servanthood for both husband and wife in more detail.)

Personal schedules will dictate what kind of service will be most helpful. If both husband and wife are working full-time outside the home, divvying up household chores may be the answer. If one's at home full-time with kids, especially preschoolers, then taking the "I'll watch the kids for a while" baton after dinner can provide an essential break at the end of an exhausting day of too many questions and dirty diapers, discipline, and simply keeping a watchful eye on wandering, inquisitive little hands and feet.

WE NEED BALANCE

*I will make him a helper **suitable** for him.*
(Genesis 2:18, emphasis added)

The need. The Genesis account records God's solution to the missing ingredient in Adam's life: "Make a helper suitable for him." What He was identifying here was the need for someone to provide *balance* in Adam's life. Left to his own devices, Adam was likely to struggle more because he lacked the perspective of that "suitable" helper. As we saw in the first chapter, God made men and women different for good reasons. You allow those reasons to strengthen your marriage when you acknowledge them and bring them to bear on the relationship. Balance is one of the best by-products of the marriage union. But it doesn't just happen.

Your role. For God to broaden our perspective and balance us, we need Him to provide a *completer,* a companion who's a little bit (at times a lot) different from us. This seems strange at first because many of us are initially attracted to someone by certain similarities. Whether it's easygoing people or athletic people or musical people, we tend to gravitate toward those with interests or personalities similar to our own.

Love, though, tends to blossom when we notice, even secretly admire, our differences. The extrovert is drawn to the introvert's listening skills because he lacks them. The introvert respects the way an extrovert is so at ease in a crowd or standing in front of a group. The spontaneous person marvels at the forethought of a disciplined planner while the planner desperately wishes she could act on a whim or "seize the moment" more often. The one who is calm under pressure is a hero to the lover who wears her emotions on her sleeve. The stoic is drawn to the transparency of one who has the freedom to ride the emotional roller coaster on occasion. Point being . . . we each need a broader set of skills, emotions, opinions, and gifts than either one of us brings to the relationship.

If you like to cook, I'm guessing your favorite recipes have a special spot in the kitchen (or in your memory), and when you pull them out you follow them to the letter. The first one I learned was for French toast. The batter comes first—a couple of eggs mixed with milk and a dash of salt, perhaps a pinch of cinnamon. Then you dunk some slices of bread in that batter and fry them in a big pan, with melted butter of course. Cook to a golden brown, plop the toast on a plate, add a little more butter, then some syrup, and it's ready to serve. But French toast alone doesn't make a balanced meal. It takes juice, maybe a little fruit, bacon if you're ignoring the calories altogether, and a cup of coffee to complete the package. In marriage, we address the need for balance by playing the role of the completer. What the one lacks, the other makes up for. The result is a complete package.

The gift. This gift takes many forms, but at its heart is the word *perspective.* We need a *different* way of looking at life and the decisions it demands of us. And I'm not talking about a *better* perspective, just a *different* one. Then together we are stronger, deeper, wiser . . . better equipped to handle whatever comes our way.

As couples make decisions, they almost always profit from the dual input of the "team." The husband, for example, will tend to be more task focused. "What's it take to get this done?" is the operative question. A wife will often add another question, something like, "How will it make them feel if we handle it this way?" Her emphasis will tend to be more relationally focused, and she'll be less inclined to develop tunnel vision.

Many men will tell you that their wives have an intuitive sense we would do well to heed when making important decisions. My friend and coauthor Jac La Tour told me that several times when he was considering career opportunities, his tendency was to look only at the positive aspects of the jobs he had been offered. When his wife Jackie injected some objectivity into the equation by pointing out some trade-offs he hadn't taken into account, Jac says he got defensive at first. Thanks to his commitment to make such significant decisions a joint effort, though, he was able to step back and evaluate all aspects of the opportunity and make a better decision.

The survey mentioned earlier found that the greatest single needs for women and men were dramatically different. For women, the number one need was to be cared for. Men, on the other hand, needed to be trusted. Because men's and women's needs differ, one of the things we must learn to do is show love in the way that the other party needs it, not in the way we need it. While we tend to love others in the way we yearn to be loved, we bring balance to a relationship when we recognize our unique differences and seek to complete our wife or husband by bringing our uniqueness to bear with her or his best interests in mind.

WE NEED ESTEEM

The man said, "This is now bone of my bones, And flesh of my flesh; she shall be called Woman, because she was taken out of Man." For this reason a man shall leave his father and his mother, and be joined to his wife; and they shall become one flesh.
(Genesis 2:23–24)

The need. If my pastoral counseling experience is an accurate gauge, it is not an exaggeration to say that there's an epidemic of low self-esteem today. Too many children and adults find it difficult to view themselves positively. Adam's response when he first laid eyes on Eve gives us a model for rectifying this problem. "This is now bone of my bones, and flesh of my flesh," he said. Rough translation: "Wow, I like you! I'm impressed." We all need to be *esteemed.* Adam recognized this at the get-go—and said so!

In my own life and ministry, what my wife Becky thinks of me carries enormous weight. Her positive evaluation of a sermon's impact, for example, means more than ten other affirming assessments combined. And if I'm waffling, hesitant to tackle a tough assignment or difficult topic, all it takes is an "I believe in you" or "You can do that" from Becky and I'm off and running.

Your role. Have you ever heard of home-court advantage? It's that phenomenon which says the home team has an edge on their competition. Why? Because their gym, arena, or stadium is filled with fans. Their fans. And nothing makes you feel like a winner more quickly than the knowledge that you've got people in your court, people who believe in you. When you assume the role of a *fan,* you automatically esteem the object of your affection.

More than one dictionary suggests that the terms *fan* and *fanatic* are related. I'm of the opinion that when it comes to our spouses, it's OK to ignore the thin line that separates the two. After all, the Latin origin of the latter term, *fanaticus,* means "inspired by divinity," so who's to say this kind of "excessive enthusiasm and intense uncritical devotion," as one dictionary defines fanatic, doesn't amount to a higher calling? One thing I know for sure is that great fans don't show up only when the team is on a roll.

It was more than thirty years after the Green Bay Packers established their dominance in the National Football League under Vince Lombardi's leadership in the mid-1960s before the team returned to the Super Bowl. Every one of those years, though, Lambeau Field sold out for home games, and the waiting list for season tickets remained thousands of names long. And people didn't just show up. They came all decked out in green and gold, rain or shine, warm and sunny, or when the wind chill factor was fifty degrees below zero. On those brutal days, some "fanatics" even came wearing little more than their cheese heads and a pair of jeans, their upper bodies and faces warmed only by a thin coat of green and gold paint and a serious case of "excessive enthusiasm and uncritical devotion." Win or lose, the Packers' fans were there cheering their team on.

The gift. An essential characteristic of fans who build esteem is that they're not just fair-weather fans. They cheer you on when you're doing well and when you're having a tough time. The gift we give on both occasions, if we're intent on building esteem, is the same. It's the gift of *praise.* If someone gives his best effort but doesn't knock the ball out of the park, the fan sees and applauds that effort. And the beauty of offering the gift of praise is that it not only builds esteem; it also bolsters confidence that the person can do even better next time.

Praise is especially powerful when it's given by the one you love the most—your husband or wife—in the presence of friends, those

43

whose opinions you value highly. You may act and even feel embarrassed, but down deep inside you'll have to admit that there's a remarkably healthy boost in your sense of personal confidence.

We have a tradition on our pastoral staff of going on an overnight getaway each year with our spouses. Part of this tradition includes honoring a member of the team for some significant contribution or simply for their value to the rest of us. Without exception, those who are put in the spotlight feel uncomfortable being there, especially at first. As they endure an appropriate dose of affirming words, though, one thing always proves true. If the person being honored is married, when his or her spouse stands to speak, the awkward smile is transformed into one of confident gratitude. It's understandable. When the one who knows you best has the floor, there's a legitimate sense that *this* person knows what he or she is talking about. So the things said sink deep in the heart . . . right where they belong.

WE NEED SECURITY

A man shall leave his father and his mother, and be joined to his wife; and they shall become one flesh. (Genesis 2:24)

The need. At the point in the Genesis text where it tells us "For this reason a man shall leave his father and his mother, and be joined to his wife; and they shall become one flesh," there's a mysterious choice of words we need to notice. Why does it say that a man shall "leave his father and his mother" when neither Adam nor Eve had parents? They were the only two people born without belly buttons. Obviously, God was laying down a principle here that we need to know. It's that when we approach marriage, we need to recognize that we're leaving a safe, secure relationship which we're to replace with a new relationship that's equally safe and *secure*. We need to know that if the going gets tough, our commitment gets tougher.

I'll never forget the story I heard of a young machinist whose hobby was restoring old cars. Just three weeks after his marriage he was welding a gas tank that he thought had been flushed and filled with water when it ignited in his face. The resulting burns were dreadfully disfiguring, but his young bride assured him that this tragedy was part of her love and commitment when she said "I do."

44

Your role. Where does that sense of security come from when a person is growing up? It flows from a home environment where the loyalty and love of Mom and Dad is unquestioned. When we say "I do" at the altar, we agree to assume this role of *loyal lover,* to provide the same sense of security that our new mate is leaving behind.

Marriage vows have traditionally conveyed the depth of commitment that would provide this sense of security. When you say "as long as we both shall live," your message is as clear as Paul's implied answer when he asked, "Who will separate us from the love of Christ?" (Romans 8:35). Just as we find "eternal security" in the assurance that Jesus is with us for the duration, so we build a similar sense of security in our marriages when we vow to stay at it until we step into eternity.

It's not uncommon these days for couples to write their own wedding vows. Some are not only beautiful but also equally clear in expressing a lifetime commitment. Others, tragically, eliminate the eternal dimension. One I heard had changed ever so slightly. The couple said, "As long as we both shall *love.*" What a difference one letter can make. The tragedy is that once the commitment becomes conditioned on how we feel, real intimacy goes out the window. How can I risk being honest when I have no sense of security that our permanent *commitment* will catch us when we fall? That would be like asking a trapeze artist to try new moves, more difficult flips, without a safety net. The result is a risky exchange—the freedom to really fly for a fear of falling.

The gift. The wedding band and vows powerfully symbolize and illustrate the kind of gift you can give to bring that needed sense of security. Your words at the altar and the rings you exchange proclaim your intentions to your spouse and to the wedding guests. The *commitment* you're making is the gift that will build a sense of security in the one to whom you're making that commitment.

I've found that building three elements into your marriage commitment communicates the sense of lifelong loyalty that we all need. They need no explanation, but they do need to be revisited regularly by way of reminder, especially when you find yourselves in conflict. Here they are:

1. Divorce is not an option.
2. Never threaten to leave.
3. When you're in conflict, reaffirm your commitment.

(We'll cover this area of commitment in chapter 9 as we examine in more depth the nature of the vows taken in marriage.)

WE NEED INTIMACY

And they shall become one flesh. (Genesis 2:24)

The need. The Genesis text puts physical *intimacy* squarely at the heart of the marriage relationship. The need to become "one flesh" was there from the outset. It is, perhaps, the most extreme aspect of man's need to be "unalone" as we discussed earlier. It is the need to know and to be known fully, to give and receive completely, the need to become entirely vulnerable and to offer genuine safeness. This need is as essential as our need for air, water, and food. When it goes unmet, our hearts get hard and our love grows cold. When we seek to fill it prematurely, outside the context of marriage, we succumb to selfishness. We say that we care more about getting than giving, more about our pleasure than another's safety. We reduce a precious gift to a hedonistic plaything. And in the process we violate the divine foundation God established for this unique institution of marriage.

Another tragedy of our culture is that too many people are either ignorant of or not interested in the differences between romance and sex. A healthy sexual relationship begins with the giving of gifts we've already mentioned. When a man gives his wife the gifts of time, a servant-spirit, perspective, praise, commitment, and (as we'll see in a moment) unconditional love, he is nurturing her soul in a way that prepares her for sexual intimacy.

Your role. Sex and romance are both wonderful gifts from God. We are free to receive them when we marry, but the key is to remember that our best response at the outset is to give them away rather than seek and demand them. The key question for both husband and wife in this regard is "What can I do to please you?"

If ever there was a role that you should seek to play, this is it. This is the lead in the marriage musical. It's the role of the *romantic lover.* Unfortunately, too many of us bring all the wrong motivations and emotions to the marriage bed. When our understanding of love is skewed or incomplete, our physical intimacy can become a tool used for all the wrong reasons. If we're angry or hurt or frustrated, physical intimacy becomes a means of manipulation. If we're selfish or insensitive or simply clueless, it becomes a road to self-gratification. If, however, it is approached with that servant-spirit we discussed earlier, your focus will be on pleasing your mate, not yourself. The beauty of this approach is that you will end up being pleased as well. Just listen to the mutual sensitivity for their loved ones that is expressed in these lines from Song of Solomon.

> *My beloved has gone down to his garden,*
> *To the beds of balsam,*
> *To pasture his flock in the gardens*
> *And gather lilies.*
> *I am my beloved's and my beloved is mine,*
> *He who pastures his flock among the lilies....*
>
> *How beautiful are your feet in sandals,*
> *O prince's daughter!*
> *The curves of your hips are like jewels,*
> *The work of the hands of an artist.*
> —Song of Solomon 6:2–3; 7:1

The gift. Our culture tries to make the role of romance the lead thing in a relationship, and consequently people get into all kinds of trouble. When we realize that it's meant to be the final act in the play, the finishing touch, rather than the opening scene, we're free to discover true freedom in this area of our lives together. It's at this point that we're able to freely give our bodies, ourselves, our *total selves,* to the one we love. *Sexual love* is a most precious gift. Interestingly, this is a gift that mirrors the depth of relationship our loving God desires to have with each one of us, and which the lonely human heart yearns for as well. Listen to what Eugene Peterson had to say about this connection as he recounted the details of a counseling appointment:

> She came to me at the recommendation of a friend. She had been troubled for years, seeing psychiatrists *seriatim* and not getting any better. The consultation had been arranged on the tele-

47

phone so that when she walked into my study it was a first meeting. Her opening statement was, "Well, I suppose you want to know all about my sex life—that's what they always want to know." I answered, "If that is what you want to talk about I'll listen. What I would really be interested in finding out about, though, is your prayer life."

She didn't think I was serious, but I was. I was interested in the details of her prayer life for the same reason that her psychiatrists had been interested in the details of her sex life—to find out how she handled intimate relationships. I had to settle for the details of her sex life at the time. Sex was the only language she knew for describing relationships of intimacy. At a later time, when she came to understand herself in relationship to a personal God, she also learned to use the language of prayer.

I like to tell the story because it juxtaposes two things that crisscross in pastoral work: sexuality and prayer. And it juxtaposes them in such a way as to show that they are both aspects of a single, created thing: a capacity for intimacy.[2]

God wants us to experience both joy and fulfillment in our sexual relationship. But realize that great sex is the result of great intimacy and love, not the cause of it. Look at it this way. Sex is a good thermometer but a lousy thermostat. It's good for measuring the warmth of a relationship but seldom able to raise the temperature in the room.

WE NEED ACCEPTANCE

And the man and his wife were both naked and were not ashamed.
(Genesis 2:25)

The need. I'm convinced that notion of nakedness goes far beyond being physically undressed. It's the idea that you're totally laid out, that there are no secrets between you and your mate, and that you can be unashamed despite having exposed yourself to that level of honesty. Each one of us needs someone with whom we can be naked yet free from shame. We need the freedom to be transparent with the assurance of acceptance. And we must remember that *acceptance* assumes the other gifts we've mentioned are present, especially security.

Your role. If you consider this notion of nakedness, an essential component for creating an atmosphere that allows it is the willingness to listen. If I'm ever going to expose my heart and soul, it's only going to happen if I know I'm free to do so and if I'm sure that I'll be heard by someone with whom I can entrust such sensitive information. Listen to what Mike Mason said in his book *The Mystery of Marriage.*

> For to be naked with another person is a sort of picture or symbolic demonstration of perfect honesty, perfect trust, perfect giving and commitment, and if the heart is not naked along with the body, then the whole action becomes a lie and a mockery.[3]

"Naked, not ashamed" relationships must also be, as Jesus was, "full of grace and truth" (John 1:14). The nakedness of truth is essential for building and maintaining trust. No secrets. Successes and failures out in the open. Without a grace-filled response we soon begin to hide our imperfections. Lies will replace truth. Masks will replace transparency; shame will create distance, avoidance, and bitterness. By playing the role of the *listening lover,* you create this atmosphere of openness and trust and invite your partner into the safety that it represents.

The gift. Given the topic under discussion here, it is entirely fitting that the final gift you have to offer is one that was first given by the Creator of planets, people, and marriage. It is the gift of *unconditional love.* Since man's fall into sin, this gift has been needed by every man and woman, and since Christ's atoning death at Calvary, it has been available to all. His unconditional love is made apparent in that "while we were yet sinners, Christ died for us" (Romans 5:8). Did you catch that? His sacrifice, His love, His sufferings occurred before we ever sought Him out and said "I'm sorry." He took the first step, a huge, giant, history-changing step from a throne in heaven to a small food trough on earth. And that was only the first night. He grew up, suffered, and mounted a cross for us. He did it while we were yet sinners. Wow! That's an unconditional love which models acceptance.

Isn't it interesting that Adam and Eve's innocence allowed them to be "naked," totally honest and exposed, and "not ashamed." But that was lost when mankind, both planets if you will, fell out of orbit around God's love and into sin. Instantly, they sensed shame and tried to cover themselves.

Then the eyes of both of them were opened, and they knew that they were naked; and they sewed fig leaves together and made themselves loin coverings. (Genesis 3:7)

They experienced shame, and when God confronted them, Adam progressed quickly from shame to blame.

The man said, "The woman whom You gave to be with me, she gave me from the tree, and I ate." (Genesis 3:12)

It was the woman's fault! That one's been around awhile, hasn't it? Not only was it her fault; it was God's fault. "The woman whom *You* gave to be with me" were Adam's words. It's as if he were saying, "Yeah, God, I didn't ask for that nap or that woman . . . see what You've caused!" Ever since that moment in history, the sexes have been naked, feeling ashamed, and blaming one another and God.

The irony is that Jesus Christ, the only One to never sin, had to hang naked and ashamed before the masses on the cross. He suffered in nakedness in order to restore our ability to come before God naked, exposed, and honest—to receive total forgiveness and unconditional acceptance. Once we taste His unconditional love and His Spirit indwells and enlivens our spirit, then we too can offer our spouse that kind of grace-filled, unconditional love and acceptance. In marriage, we can again be naked and unashamed.

As a consequence of what Christ did, for those who receive this unconditional love, "God is not ashamed to be called their God" (Hebrews 11:16). What better gift can we give the woman or man we love than this same measure of love—unconditional love.

Genesis 1–2 provides a great introduction to marriage, so don't be surprised when you see these seven gifts resurface in the passages we'll be studying later on. They're foundational concepts on which we'll be building. And just in case you think I'm naive, I realize that what we've been talking about here is God's ideal. And right about now you may be thinking, "Yeah, Dale, this is the ideal, but I live in an ordeal, and I want a new deal." I'm hearing you. After all, the next verse of our Genesis text is clear: "Now the serpent was more crafty than any beast of the field" (Genesis

3:1). Even though men and women were different by design, those differences were not the real problem, at least not initially. They added strength and spice to the relationship. They were cause for appreciation and celebration, not division and conflict. So what happened? Man sinned. And immediately the conflict, the blaming, and the shaming began. However, God still had a plan for restoration.

So turn the page and let's talk about how to turn an ordeal into a new deal.

NOTES

1. John Gray, *Men Are from Mars, Women Are from Venus* (New York: Harper-Collins, 1992), 47, emphasis added.
2. Eugene Peterson, *Five Smooth Stones for Pastoral Work* (Atlanta, Ga.: John Knox, 1980), 27–28.
3. Mike Mason, *The Mystery of Marriage* (Portland, Oreg.: Multnomah, 1985), 117.

CHAPTER THREE

THE "UNIVERSE-ALL" EQUALIZER: A SERVANT'S HEART

As we leave the Garden of Eden, Adam and Eve are on the move, not just to a new home with a new garden but to a whole new life. Gone are the days of freedom from sin and selfishness. Both man and woman, as different as they are, must now learn to live together on a sin-scarred planet. How will they fulfill the seven needs highlighted in Creation? Will they be able to assume their roles?

Throughout the rest of this book, we will explore God's master plan for bringing Mars and Venus down to earth, His distinctives for building healthy relationships on an unhealthy planet. The Creator not only understood Adam and Eve in all their glory and perfection, He knew the implications of their tragic fall into sin. Yet even with that knowledge, He wasn't about to quit on mankind or on marriage. Just as He had a plan to save and restore their souls, He had a plan to save and restore the joy of marriage.

Fast-forward with me to the New Testament. Why? Because just as the Cross is central to understanding God's grand plan of salvation, so also is it foundational to God's master plan for marriage. And although we will see in coming chapters that husbands and wives were designed to fulfill their roles in different ways, one assignment is common to both. It lays the foundation on which both can build. What is this element that's so essential to the success of our marriage mission? *Servanthood.* Our model is Jesus Christ, and His clearest demonstration of this essential came at the Cross.

Servant-love is to marriage what the concept of *lift* is to aeronautics. Without it we won't even get off the ground. By applying it, husbands and wives can be freed to welcome the undiluted blessing of God on their marriage. Yes, this is one of the more difficult maneuvers to master in this journey, but it is also one of the most rewarding.

When our children were small, they used to sing a little song called "Make Me a Servant." It caught my attention every time the kids sang it:

> Make me a servant, humble and meek.
>
> Lord, help me lift up those who are weak.
>
> And may the prayer of my heart always be:
>
> Make me a servant, make me a servant,
>
> make me a servant today.[1]

Each time I found this tune floating around the house, I smiled. For two reasons. The obvious one is that it's true, and every dad smiles when his kids speak the truth. A second reason for my smiling, though, always tempered the first, and it was that I knew from hard experience that this particular bit of truth was like a New Year's resolution: easily spoken but difficult to do. The children would discover this soon enough . . . just as Becky and I and every other couple do after we get married.

Nowhere is the lofty desire to serve another person brought more quickly down to earth than in marriage. Too many couples have crash-landed because they couldn't execute this simple-sounding command. Nevertheless, the success of a marriage mission rests heavily on a couple's ability to put this bit of wisdom into practice. After all, Paul's words to the Philippian Christians, though applicable to all of life, bear special significance for men and women who are living in such close quarters every day. The more intimate the relationship, the more important a servant-spirit becomes. As you read these verses, envision your marriage through this new paradigm for love.

Do nothing from selfishness or empty conceit, but with humility of mind regard one another as more important than yourselves; do not merely look out for your own personal interests, but also for the interests of others. (Philippians 2:3–4)

So the question is, can those of us who are happily circling in our respective orbits find in this command from mission control the wherewithal to change course and start flying together? The answer is yes, and I think the key is found in the words of Sir Arthur Keith, who once said, "The course of human history is determined, not by what happens in the skies, but by what takes place in the hearts of men."

It is in the heart—the seat of our intellect, our feelings, and our will—that we invite the Lord of the universe to do that special work which will equip us to launch into a life of service to the one we love. When it comes to living in marriage, what husbands need in themselves and at the center of their marriage union is the heart of a servant. And, yes, the same holds true for wives. It'll take a servant's heart to pull off their unique, God-given assignments as well.

Now, servanthood can take very different forms, depending on the servant and the servant's objectives. Some servants in New Testament times were overworked and undervalued "possessions." Others were highly valued, well educated, working as private tutors, and loved like a part of the family. The dress and daily routines of servants were radically different from one another, but at the core of their lives, they were all still slaves. My point is that no matter how the husband looks and acts in his role, he'll only be effective if he has the heart of a servant. Likewise for the wife. A servant's heart is the prime directive no matter what shape her roles and responsibilities take day by day. To be what God demands, spouses must first be servants. This requirement is at the core of both of their job descriptions.

Your goal in serving is to meet the other person's needs. To do that, you must first identify and understand those needs.

You'll find a great example of this heart of service if you happen to find yourself in one of the Ritz-Carlton's luxurious hotels. I'm told that if you walk up to any employee and ask for directions to some part of the hotel, you will not be given those directions. Instead, you'll be personally escorted to your destination by a smiling worker who has been instructed to stop whatever he or she is doing at that moment and take you where you wish to go. That's the kind of servant-spirit we're talking about.

Before we explore this idea further, let's look again at the master plan to determine what is the essence of a servant-heart and then examine the supreme example we all need to follow.

THE ESSENCE OF A SERVANT-HEART

Paul's words in Philippians 2:3–4 are a paradigm for all of life and human relationships that explains the essence of genuine servanthood. It begins with an attitude. That attitude then manifests itself in action. Paul's paradigm lays a great foundation for marriage. His words reveal two radically different approaches to life. Every moment of every day other people pass into my orbit, my "space." When it comes to marriage, we're called to inhabit the same orbit for life. What Paul said is that my response is determined not only by what I think of others in my orbit, but what I think of myself. Check out this chart with key phrases from this passage.

OUR PRIORITIES		
MY ATTITUDE	Conceit	Humility
PERSPECTIVE	Selfishness	Others More Important
FOCUS/CONCERN	Personal Interests	Interests of Others
ACTIONS	Serve Me!	Serve Others!

If my spirit is conceited, I'm constantly whispering things to myself like "Man, am I something . . . I wonder if she (or he) realizes how fortunate she is to have me around . . . I deserve better than this . . . What would he do without me? . . . I've really got it together . . . I know I'm right." That spirit of *conceit* sets me on a certain course. Just follow the chart downward as I fall from my orbit. My perspective will be me focused. *Selfishness* is what the Bible calls it. I am the supreme person in my universe. That perspective draws my focus to my "own *personal interests*" as I subconsciously look out for number one. My prime objective is to *be served,* to use people to advance my agenda. Is this not the core issue in most marital conflicts?

This is why we spend so much time in premarital counseling helping couples better understand themselves and each other. If things such as personality traits, defense mechanisms, and learned behaviors can be identified early on, couples can talk through their differences, recognize potential trouble spots, and even make decisions to change for their own good and the good of their marriage.

Fortunately, there is hope. There's an alternative paradigm— one of servant-marriage. It, too, starts with an attitude, this time one of *humility.* Now there's a word you don't see thrown around much these days. My friend's 1950 edition of *Webster's New International Dictionary* has a lot to say about this wonderful word. "State or quality of being humble in spirit," it says. "Freedom from pride and arrogance." It even lists the King James rendering of this concept: "lowliness of mind." My favorites, though, are the secondary definitions listed there: "an act of submission" and "humble courtesy."

This kind of attitude produces a dramatically different perspective, namely that *others* really are important, even *more important* than myself at times. My focus shifts to an intentional choice to "look out . . . for the *interests of others.*" The servant-lover, male or female, looks to this attitude of humility to guide his or her actions.

Paul cautioned us strongly by saying we should "do *nothing* from selfishness or empty conceit" (emphasis added). This conceit, if I'm reading Paul correctly, actually leads to selfishness, just as humility very naturally prompts us to regard others as equally important, in some cases, more important than ourselves. If I take Paul's words to heart and start changing the way I think, it follows quite naturally that my way of living will begin to change as well. The thought that I'm to regard others as more important than myself, as it becomes a conviction of my heart, will tend to turn selfish behavior into servant behavior. How do I know when my attitude of conceit is shifting to one of humility? When I find myself looking out *not only* for my own needs but also for the needs of others, especially those of my spouse, my children, or my friends.

The servant-lover sees a need and simply does it. Seldom does this quality demand a major sacrifice, although it can. More often it consists of daily little acts that sweeten the relationship a little at a time. I once asked some friends the question, "When do you see your spouse as a servant?" Here's what they said:

> He folds the towels after they're dry . . . my way, not his.
> She eats the burned toast . . . every time.
> He fixes the coffee . . . then wakes me.
> She goes to the Dodger game with me.
> He empties the dishwasher.
> She drops the kids at the movie.
> He picks up the kids from the movie.
> He returns almost-overdue videos at 11:55 P.M.
> She lets the dog out . . . again.
> He lets the dog in . . . again.
> He gives me the car . . . even when it leaves him stranded.
> She gets up at 5:00 A.M. to taxi one of the kids somewhere
>   . . . while I sleep in.

All of us need to live like servants. The issue is, whom are we willing to serve? Every one of us serves other people every day. It's inevitable. For some, the list of who gets served is a short one; for others it's longer, but one thing holds constant: We decide who gets on that list. If my decision is based on conceit, I'll be self-focused, I'll be looking out for number one, and that will be evident to all who observe my life. What they'll see is a selfish guy who is known for taking rather than giving, for using without appreciating, for hoarding instead of sharing. Conversely, if a humble heart is driving my decision, what the world will see is . . . a servant . . . one who gives, who appreciates, who shares. In a word, one who loves.

THE BEST EXAMPLE OF A SERVANT-HEART

For many of us, Philippians 2:3–4 sounds great, but it's just too, well, theoretical. Can you show us what it looks like? That's our question. We need a mentor, a model of real servanthood.

Once again, God delivered! Because this living out of our attitude has such a dramatic effect on our marriage, it's in the best interests of both members of the flight crew to have a sound illustration of what the servant-heart in action looks like. The following few verses provide this essential example.

> *Have this attitude in yourselves which was also in Christ Jesus, who, although He existed in the form of God, did not regard equality with God a thing to be grasped, but emptied Himself, taking the form of a bond-servant, and being made in the likeness of men. Being found in appearance as a man, He humbled Himself by becoming obedient to the point of death, even death on a cross. For this reason also, God highly exalted Him, and bestowed on Him the name which is above every name, so that at the name of Jesus every knee will bow, of those who are in heaven and on earth and under the earth, and that every tongue will confess that Jesus Christ is Lord, to the glory of God the Father. (Philippians 2:5–11)*

Jesus, the One who did not come to be served but to serve, is the example we need to follow. He's the epitome of servant-hearted love. And in these verses we find no less than seven facets of His example, seven ways that He modeled servanthood to those whose worlds can seem so far apart. By the way, take note that "serving" is not restricted to women and children. Jesus Christ was both a real man and a servant, the model servant of all time. The word *servant* is not synonymous with terms like *fake, wimp, weak, insecure, indecisive, people pleaser,* or *victim.*

It's not for fakes . . . because it's spirit driven. When Paul said to "have this *attitude in yourselves* which was also in Christ Jesus" (Philippians 2:5, emphasis added; so throughout), he was laying the foundation for servant-hearted living. Don't focus first on behavior. Check the attitude that's driving how you behave. If it always demands that you go to the front of the line, it's time for an attitude adjustment. The servant who honors God is real, genuine, authentic, and serving from the heart of humility. No actors or fakes allowed; only real men and women should report for duty. If a husband or wife is putting on the mask of a servant without the heart, the charade will break down under pressure.

It's not for weaklings . . . because serving is a powerful thing. Despite modern misconceptions, being a servant does not mean relegating yourself to a position of weakness. This Jesus, who "although He *existed* in the *form of God,*" was certainly no pushover. His was not a powerless role, and neither is yours when you choose to serve your spouse. As a servant, you operate from a position of strength because you're following the example of the all-powerful One who "existed in the form of God." The best servants are those who know their strengths and know what they have to offer their spouses. The beauty is that service of this sort strengthens the marriage as well. The goal of a servant-husband or wife is to use whatever gifts, abilities, power, or position you possess to support and serve your spouse.

It's not for the insecure . . . because it's about security. To serve well, a servant must be secure, not second-guessing, not perpetually wondering or worrying about what others are thinking. Jesus possessed this kind of assurance. When the text says that He "*did not regard* equality with God a thing to be grasped," we get a glimpse of One who knew Himself and His mission. He didn't need the accolades and praise of others. As long as He was pursuing the will of His Father, pleasing Him, Jesus was secure. It's as if He was saying, "Yes, I'm God. And no, they don't see the whole picture, but it doesn't matter." Why? Because Jesus' position in the Godhead provided all the security He needed. He trusted the One whom He ultimately served and knew that to obey Him was the only way to go. Because of this, He neither had to flaunt His deity, nor was He concerned about what other people thought about Him. Knowing that He was pleasing God was all the security He needed, and when you're toughing it out during the dry or dreary or difficult days of your marriage, it's all the security you need too. The secure husband can humbly serve his wife and not worry about what the world thinks of him. Likewise, the secure wife can respectfully follow the leadership of her husband even if her friends don't understand or agree.

It's not for the indecisive . . . because it's about choosing to serve. A lot of people think serving is analogous to being taken advantage of, that it's a decision to become subservient to someone else. But when we read that "He *emptied* Himself, taking the form of a bond-servant," we learn something different, something opposite. Serving is not about *being taken; it's about choosing to give.* Servants like Jesus willingly suspend their rights, privileges, time, and agendas to meet their spouses' needs. Unlike slaves, whose lives of servility are forced upon them, spouses who follow Jesus' example make a deliberate decision to serve. When a husband sacrifices a round of golf to make the rounds at the mall with his wife, he should rejoice in his decision to place his wife and her needs ahead of his own. Servants learn to make tough choices.

It's not for the self-possessed . . . because it's about exploring my spouse's world to discover his or her needs. Paul told the Philippians that Jesus, "being made in the likeness of men" and "being *found* in appearance as a man," *humbled* Himself. Think about it. This is God Incarnate we're talking about here. God in the flesh. But instead of arriving on earth with public proclamations that this is His world, He came as a man, a common man. He learned to understand our needs, feel our pain, share our joy—you could say He learned our language. Good servants do well to follow His example. Too often we fail to serve our spouses because we don't take the time to learn their language. The way men and women think and process things can be dramatically different. You need to enter your spouse's world and learn about those differences.

For example, I tell couples in counseling to become students of their spouses. In fact, as part of this unique flight crew, make this one class you excel in. I hope someday to have a doctorate in "Rebecology," the discipline and study of Rebecca Susan Burke. Could you write a term paper on your spouse? Here's an outline to get you started.

- Ancestors
- Parents and grandparents (beliefs, habits, values, major events of their lives)
- Early life/formative years
- Top ten events that shaped them
- Teen years
- Favorite vacations
- Greatest regrets
- Greatest dreams fulfilled; unfulfilled
- Top five disappointments
- Top five accomplishments
- Five trips they'd love to take before they die
- Struggles and obstacles of today
- Spiritual journey

- Spiritual gifts and passions
- Complete the following:
  "Before I die I want to . . ."
  "I feel loved when you . . ."
  "One thing I'd love for you to change . . ."

This is quite a course of study, isn't it? Why bother undertaking it? Because great servants know the one they serve . . . intimately.

It's not for victims . . . because it's about being a victor. Frequently when I counsel couples, a common concern crops up. It sounds like this: "But, Dale, if I take this servant thing seriously, my husband/wife is going to walk all over me. I'll just be a doormat." Now, if that were true, I wouldn't want any part of it either. There's absolutely nothing exciting about being a doormat. You just sort of lie around all day waiting to be stepped on. But serving Jesus' way does not demand that you become a doormat. In fact, verse 8 says it's exactly the opposite of becoming a victim. Jesus became *obedient* to the point of death, even death on a cross. We take our cue from Him. Paul was saying that Jesus became a *willing* sacrifice. What's even more remarkable is that He came obediently to serve, knowing that this outcome awaited Him. But He didn't just sit around waiting for it to come to Him. Jesus engaged His earthly life, and the outcome was the promise of eternal life for you and me. By becoming a willing sacrifice, He secured victory for those He came to serve. Always remember—the difference between a victim and a servant is as pronounced as the contrast between a doormat and a sacrifice. The doormat is a loser, but the one who willingly lays down his life for another is a hero. When we as men and women choose to lay it all on the line to serve the one we love, God honors our sacrificial, servant-love.

Just ask the woman who worked to put her husband through medical school, or the guy who skipped a promotion and job transfer because his wife and kids said the move wasn't in the best interests of the family, or the woman who worked as a nurse to help put her husband through seminary. That woman, by the way, is my wife Becky, and God has honored me through her sacrifice.

It's not for people pleasers . . . because it's about pleasing God. Verses 9–11 do us a great service by bringing the previous verses into focus. When Paul wrote that "God highly exalted Him, and bestowed on Him the name which is above every name," he was very clear to communicate the reason for Jesus' being elevated to this position of prominence. Everyone will confess that "Jesus Christ is Lord," he said, not for Jesus' glory alone, but *to the glory of God the Father.*" When Jesus gave His body and shed His blood for us, He wasn't doing it simply to please people. He wasn't concerned only with meeting our need for a savior. We have cause every day to thank Him that He did meet our need in this regard; but, ultimately, He served us in this way as an act of obedience to His heavenly Father. Jesus was driven to please God.

There's a valuable application here for couples, for many times, when you try to be a servant in marriage, the question of motivation flashes up on your control panel. You see, if I'm serving strictly to please my spouse, or if my motive in serving is simply to get my mate to serve me, I'm in trouble over the long haul. What happens if I give and don't get back? Chances are better than even that pretty soon I'll stop giving. I've seen it happen over and over. If, on the other hand, my primary motive is to glorify God through the way I love and serve my wife, then even if she doesn't respond, I keep serving. I know my Father in heaven is pleased with how I'm treating her. And if my greatest motivation is to please my God and Savior, then I can keep on serving, keep on loving, keep on giving, knowing that my reward may never come on this planet. My perseverance also boosts the likelihood that my spouse will eventually take notice and respond in kind. Can I be sure? No way. But I know that my marriage will be enriched as a result.

At this point, you may be wrestling with an apparent incongruity. You're inclined to agree with what we've discussed, but you're concerned that the Philippians text wasn't written specifically about marriage. As we explore further in chapter 4, I hope you'll see that not only does this text apply to marriage, but that the idea of the servant-spirit undergirds every other biblical teaching about marriage.

Just how far are we to carry this business of "not merely looking out for your own personal interests"? Are we to serve one another in the marriage relationship even to the point of radical sacrifice? I think the wife of the prominent Los Angeles Pastor E. V. Hill took it that seriously.

You may recall the terrible days in the mid-1960s when rioting ravaged the city of Watts near Los Angeles. At the peak of the violence, Dr. Hill made the difficult decision to denounce from the pulpit his neighbors who were destroying property and stealing from local stores and shops. Not surprisingly, this brand of preaching brought threats to this courageous pastor and his church. Nevertheless, as the lawbreaking intensified, so did his public condemnation of the rioters.

One evening the phone rang in the pastor's home. Dr. Hill answered but hung up quickly without saying a word. Mrs. Hill noticed, though, that his face was strained, somber.

"What was that all about?" she asked.

"Oh, nothing," replied Dr. Hill, unconvincingly. But his wife kept pressing, and he finally told her, "They have threatened to blow up our car with me in it." Late into that night they talked about how it would be impossible for them to protect their car from wire bombings.

The next morning, when Dr. Hill walked into the kitchen he noticed that his wife was, uncharacteristically, not in the house. Neither was his car in the carport, which prompted significant concern on his part. But a few minutes later he saw the car roll into the driveway with his wife at the wheel. She had driven around the block to make sure it would be safe for her husband to drive later on that morning.

That, my friend, is sacrificial love. True servant-love. No wonder Dr. Hill said, "From that day, I have never wondered if my wife loved me."

Mrs. Hill's actions communicated loudly and clearly to her husband her understanding of Paul's paradigm: "Do not merely look out for your own personal interests, but also for the interests of *your spouse*." How about in your home? How do you communicate your love to your mate? What does it take to transmit the all-important message, "I love you"? We'll explore this frontier in the next chapter.

NOTE

1. Kelly Willard, "Make Me a Servant." Copyright © 1982 WILLING HEART MUSIC (Administered By MARANATHA! MUSIC c/o THE COPYRIGHT COMPANY, Nashville, TN) MARANATHA! MUSIC (Administered By THE COPYRIGHT COMPANY, Nashville, TN) All Rights Reserved. International Copyright Secured. Used By Permission.

CHAPTER FOUR

HOW DO
MEN SAY
"I LOVE YOU"?

From the moment men and women arrived on Planet Earth, two things have been true. One is that "God created man in His own image, . . . male and female He created them" (Genesis 1:27). Every person born is identical in this regard. We all bear the image of our Creator. The other verity is that men and women are different. As we learned in chapter 1, when God said, "It is not good for the man to be alone; I will make him a helper suitable for him" (Genesis 2:18), He was identifying man's need for one who could complete him, one who was created significantly different from the man—for a reason.

People have been observing these differences for centuries, and some have recently taken to compiling lists of their observations. One list I came across, likely compiled by a group of first grade girls at a slumber party, highlights thirty- one of these distinctions. A few of my favorites follow.

Girls Are More Better Than Boys

1. Girls chew with their mouths closed.
2. Girls don't pick their noses.

3. Girls go to the bathroom politely.
4. Girls don't smell as bad.
5. Girls are more smarter.
6. Girls shave more.
7. Girls have more manners.

Not to be outdone, one anonymous male came up with a list of thirty-nine advantages to being a man. Why thirty-nine? I don't know for sure, but my guess is that he read the list of "thirty-one" and wasn't content to just match it. After all, guys hate for contests to end in a tie. Here are some of his thirty-nine "Reasons to Be a Man."

1. Phone conversations are over in thirty seconds flat.
2. A five-day vacation requires only one suitcase.
3. You get extra credit for the slightest act of thoughtfulness.
4. If someone forgets to invite you to something, he or she can still be your friend.
5. You can quietly enjoy a ride from the passenger's seat.
6. Gray hair and wrinkles only add character.
7. You are not expected to know the names of more than five colors.

We all laugh at these differences between the genders, but there's more truth in both lists than we'd like to admit. Men and women really are different from one another in so many ways. Some, even most, seem rather trivial, but these "trivial" differences have at times ignited conflicts that escalated into all-out warfare and even divorce.

The stakes go up substantially when we try to answer the question "When do you feel loved?" One researcher attempted to answer that most basic of questions from both the male and female perspectives. Dr. John Gray has both counseled couples and conducted relationship seminars. His findings were based on his counseling experience and on his questioning of the more than twenty-five-thousand people who have attended his seminars. He identified twelve kinds of love, which he broke down into the following primary love needs of women and men. This is how it would look if you arranged this information into a chart.

TWELVE KINDS OF LOVE

Women Need to Receive	Men Need to Receive
1. Caring	1. Trust
2. Understanding	2. Acceptance
3. Respect	3. Appreciation
4. Devotion	4. Admiration
5. Validation	5. Approval
6. Reassurance	6. Encouragement

My intent here is not to assess Dr. Gray's conclusions, but to point out that the lists for men and women are radically different. He said that though men and women respond at some level to the items on both lists, the primary needs expressed by the two sexes are not the same. Of special interest are the summary statements in *Men Are from Mars, Women Are from Venus*. His conclusions differ sharply from much of what is being written about marriage today by secular authors. Interestingly, though, they sound surprisingly similar to some advice given to men and women thousands of years before survey methodologies and therapists appeared on the scene. In the New Testament book of Ephesians, God's Word declares:

Husbands ought also to love their own wives as their own bodies. He who loves his own wife loves himself; for no one ever hated his own flesh, but nourishes and cherishes it, just as Christ also does the church. (Ephesians 5:28–29)

and

Wives, be subject to your own husbands, as to the Lord. . . . and the wife must see to it that she respects her husband. (Ephesians 5:22, 33)

Dr. Gray's findings seem to corroborate the Scriptures, which, if I'm reading these texts correctly, are saying simply that *men feel loved when they're respected and women feel loved when they're cared for.* These are the primary needs of men and women. Once again, we discover that the God of creation was light-years ahead of man's wisdom. He knew best how to communicate love to men, and He knew it was very different from the love language spoken by women. So God gave husbands and wives two different lists of commands. Each one, if followed, will help to meet the unique emotional needs of the opposite sex. As we saw in chapter 3, a servant-heart is the foundation for both lists, the call to serve one another in love. But the servant-style of the husband will at times be as different from his wife's as the Big Dipper is from the constellation Orion. We'll devote the rest of this chapter to examining God's commands to men; in the next chapter, we'll see what He says to women.

APPLYING A SERVANT-HUSBAND'S HEART

I'm guessing it will not surprise you that none of the lists we read earlier are original, because after God landed us on this planet, He not only built distinctives into each one of us; He also included the specifications for these differences in His master plan. And as we are about to discover, the same servant-spirit we've been discussing, which the Creator established as the model for both men and women from the beginning, was intended to be expressed in different ways by men and women. The way I apply my servant-heart to say "I love you" to my wife Becky is intentionally different from the way she'll apply hers to express her love for me.

To set the stage for our study, we need some perspective, so here's the complete list of specifications, God's lists for servant-hearted lovers.

SERVANT-HEARTED LOVERS

As a Servant-Wife, She . . .	As a Servant-Husband, He . . .
1. Respects	1. Sacrifices
2. Trusts	2. Nourishes
3. Supports	3. Cherishes
4. Accepts	4. Honors
5. Admires	5. Understands

These specs are found in several sections of God's master plan. We'll get to the ones pertaining to men in a moment. But before you prepare for takeoff, gentlemen, it's important that you understand the context in which your role is to be lived out. How are you to apply your servant-spirit on your wife's behalf?

> *For the husband is the head of the wife, as Christ also is the head of the church, He Himself being the Savior of the body. But as the church is subject to Christ, so also the wives ought to be to their husbands in everything. Husbands, love your wives, just as Christ also loved the church and gave Himself up for her.* (Ephesians 5:23–25)

To live out the high calling of a husband, men, you must assume the role of a *servant-leader*. The text clearly states that the husband "is the head of the wife." Unfortunately, extreme interpretations of this text have obscured its intended meaning. Some have said that it has absolutely nothing to do with authority. This is not true. Paul was speaking here of a leadership role for the husband. His emphasis was on how that role is to be carried out. The appropriate model is Jesus Christ. (We'll address this issue briefly here, but because it is so crucial to our understanding of men's and women's roles in a marriage relationship, we're going to study it in more depth in the next chapter.)

The husband is to lead by following Jesus' example, which means His leadership is not as a dictator, which is the spin our culture puts on the leader's role. He's the boss. He makes all the decisions. He's superior to those he leads. This is not the biblical model for leadership. The Ephesians text says that Jesus Christ is our leadership model. We're to lead as He leads, as a servant.

A common misunderstanding of this text suggests that the reference to the husband as the "head" means only that he is the source of the woman, like the headwaters of a river are its source. This view became popular a few years ago, but solid biblical scholarship affirms that the apostle Paul's reference to being the head is indeed, as we have just mentioned, one of leadership. We will save a more thorough discussion of the issues surrounding the concepts of *headship* and *submission* for chapter 5.

Flowing from this misinterpretation is the suggestion that husbands and wives are coleaders in the home. It's true that teamwork is essential for success in marriage. Without it, worlds either drift apart or collide. In fact, we affirmed in chapter 1 that men and women were created as equals. However, the issue here is not one of equality. It's a matter of responsibility. And the apostle Paul was making clear that responsibility is central to the man's role as the servant-leader. Just as Jesus takes responsibility for the needs of the church, so He expects the husband to take responsibility for the needs of the home. In saying this, we're also acknowledging the husband's responsibility to exercise initiative. If things at home are not as they should be, men, it's your responsibility to get the ball rolling. When our relationship with the Savior was estranged, Jesus took the initiative by landing in our world. We're told to follow His example.

So the context in which men are to love their wives is as servant-leaders. Keep this in mind as we explore each item on the servant-husband's list of ways to lead and love his wife.

A SERVANT-HUSBAND SACRIFICES

Topping the list is probably the most difficult assignment of all. A husband sacrifices for his wife. When we read that Jesus "gave Himself up for" the church, we're faced with the reality that authentic servant leadership is sacrificial. I love the fact that God calls us to love our wives this way. One author's paraphrase of this text is that "Christ wants us as men to always try to be first to the cross" when it comes to sacrificing for our wives. This is the mark of one who leads by caring rather than controlling.

Does the word *sacrifice* throw you off a little? It sure isn't the typical term used to describe relationships these days. How about this definition from the *American Heritage Dictionary:*

> Sacrifice is the forfeiture of something highly valued for the sake of someone or something considered to have greater value.[1]

Isn't that a great statement? It really captures the essence of servant-hearted love in a marriage. It's saying that we're to incur a loss in the transaction as we give ourselves for our wives. Imagine how your love would grow and your marriage would strengthen if every day you looked for ways, large and small, to give up things you value for your wife. And I'm talking here about things that cost you something.

Like the Monday I had told my wife Becky that we'd spend my day off doing whatever she wanted to do. Tops on her list is biking, so we'd planned a ride to the beach, about a twenty-five-mile round-trip trek from our home. It had been several weeks since we'd been able to ride together, so I promised Beck that we'd go this particular day. I was genuinely looking forward to the ride, not because I like biking as much as Becky does, but because I love being with her.

Well, just about the time we were dressed and heading out the door, the phone rang.

"Hello, Pastor Dale," the caller said.

"Yes."

"I don't know if you're interested, but I have four Lakers tickets for this afternoon's game. It's at one o'clock. I can't make afternoon games, so the tickets are yours if you can use them."

Now you have to know that I grew up a Jerry West fan. He came from a tiny West Virginia town not far from my hometown of Hurricane. So I'm also a huge Lakers fan. And at that point, I had never been to one of their home games at the Forum in Inglewood. So I'm salivating. But . . .

"You know," I replied, "I promised Becky we'd go for a bike ride today, so I'll have to pass. Maybe another time. But thanks anyway." And I hung up the phone. When I walked back outside, Becky asked who had called. And when I told her about the tickets, she quickly asked, "Well, did you take them?"

"Well, no, sweetheart. I told him that I had promised you we'd go for a bike ride."

"You know, honey, that was really sweet," she said. "But it was really dumb too."

"What?" I said, a little surprised.

"We can go for a bike ride anytime. Call him back and get those tickets!"

Besides being funny, this story turned out to be a legitimate illustration of how a marriage works when both of you are willing to give up something highly valued for the sake of the other, whom you consider to be of greater value. When both husband and wife have that spirit, the marriage ends up being the winner.

A SERVANT-HUSBAND NOURISHES

In verses 26–29 Paul explained why men are to love their wives sacrificially the way Jesus loved the church:

So that He might sanctify her, having cleansed her by the washing of water with the word, that He might present to Himself the church in all her glory, having no spot or wrinkle or any such thing; but that she would be holy and blameless. So husbands ought also to love their own wives as their own bodies. He who loves his own wife loves himself; for no one ever hated his own flesh, but nourishes and cherishes it, just as Christ also does the church. (Ephesians 5:26–29)

The Greek word rendered "nourish" is *ektrepho,* which means to feed, to bring up, to care for. You love your wife, men, by caring for her. Sometimes it's translated "to pamper" or "to rear." What Paul was talking about here is meeting the needs of the other person, helping that person grow to maturity. The idea is that you want your wife to blossom.

Men, at the risk of blowing your circuits, I think what's pictured here is a bridal attendant. You see, this text tells us that the church is what? The bride of Christ. Remember that. And Christ is like the groom. The idea is that a good husband is to be about the business of attending to the needs of his wife, of helping her become all that God wants her to be.

Have you ever been in one of those little bride's rooms before a wedding? It's a scary experience. I mean, the attendants are fussing over every little detail, every bit of hair, making sure it's all . . . perfect. And the bride is just kind of standing there, uptight, maybe dabbing the perspiration off her forehead as these attendants all flutter around her. Especially the bride's mother. That's where she's been, you know, before you see an usher escorting her down the aisle just before the ceremony begins. All her efforts, and those of every other attendant, are focused on trying to help the bride be her very best for that moment when she meets her groom.

The application of this image to marriage is really quite simple. The groom, the husband, is called to help his bride reach her full potential before she meets her Savior. If you're a husband now or about to become one, remember that this is how you're to view yourself.

If you tell your wife that your intent is to nourish her, to care for her as your own body, you're making a statement of radical love to her. (OK, I'm assuming here that you're in the habit of taking care of yourself—and that you'll exercise your senses of timing and tact. I would not, for example, recommend that you tell your wife of your intent to care for her like your own body when you're sitting on the couch watching an NHL hockey game, eating some chips, and slugging down a sixteen-ounce soda.) Follow up your words with caring behavior and your wife will know you mean business. It's one thing, for instance, to say, "Honey, I will care for your needs," but another to grab the grocery list and run to the store because she's exhausted from a day at work or from three days of caring for a sick toddler.

To nourish her is to do whatever is necessary to see her become all God wants her to be, spiritually, emotionally, intellectually, and physically. What a radical way to lead and love this special woman God has dropped into your life! Your mission in life is not just to be, as they say in the army, "all that you can be." Your assignment, men, if you are man enough to take it on, is to help your wife be "all that *she* can be." Bottom line, men, if she's not healthy and growing as a woman of God, it's your job to nourish that growth.

A SERVANT-HUSBAND CHERISHES

Nourishing and cherishing are similar, but significantly different. The Greek word for "cherish," *thalpo,* can mean "to heat" or "to soften by heat," or it can mean "to keep warm" the way birds keep their young warm by covering them with their feathers. Isn't that a tender image? It's the image we're to have in our minds, men, when we think of taking care of our wives.

What do these images mean to us today? Nothing more or less than to hold dear and to value highly. Cherishing is saying to your wife, "You're number one." It goes beyond just meeting her needs. It's also tuning in to who she is and saying with your words and actions, "You're precious. You're special."

I found it easiest to understand the difference between nourishing and cherishing when I spent time growing up with a friend whose dad was a raccoon hunter. Out behind this guy's house was a series of doghouses for Dad's coonhounds. Each one had bowls for food and water and a chain long enough to give the dog room to exercise. But they had this other dog—I called him Old Blue— who was the patriarch of all the dogs. Old Blue lived in the house. Oh, he had food and water dishes like the other dogs. But at night he wasn't chained out by a doghouse. He'd lie by the fire in the big house. Sometimes he'd lay his head in his master's lap, which would prompt Dad to rub Old Blue's ears and stroke his head.

All of those coonhounds were nourished. Their needs were met. But Old Blue was cherished. So men, the next time you sit on the couch with your wife and she lays her head against your shoulder, do something special to communicate that she is that special someone in your life. Maybe that means stroking her hair . . . or holding her close . . . or even rubbing her ears!

If you tell your wife that you choose to cherish her, you're saying she's your top priority. Nothing means more to a man's wife than to let her know there's no one ahead of her on the list of people who matter most. Yes, we're all agreed that our relationship with the Creator is paramount. That's as firmly fixed as the stars in a night sky. What we're talking about here is the nature of your priorities in the daily world of relationships and the demands of life. Make sure your wife knows where she stands on that list. Tell her with your mouth—often—that you count it a privilege to have her as your wife.

In preparation for a series I preached some years ago on marriage, we interviewed some couples in our church who had been married fifty years or more to find out the keys to their longevity, success, and joy together. Listen to what they had to say.

"If you marry an angel, it's easy! She's beautiful, she's faithful. . . . She cooks great pies!"

"Looking back, if I had to do it over again, I would be more concerned with being a helpmate to my wife and let the Lord take care of the other areas."

Isn't that a great tip? Cherish as well as nourish. Both are essential for a servant-husband who is intent on loving his wife Jesus' way. If you want a picture to help you see the difference between the two, guys, think of it like this. It's the contrast between having a routine oil change done on a company car and spending time polishing that '56 T-Bird, that treasure that's parked in the garage. There's a big difference between the special treatment a guy gives something he deems to be of value versus the routine care he gives something he merely owns. We need both. Every marriage requires routine maintenance to stay in good working order. Part of it comes from the care that's involved in nourishing your wife. But cherishing is essential as well, doing those special things, small and not so small, that communicate that vital message, "You, above all others, are special." A few more comments by the couples we just heard from make the point.

"He loves me and shows his love to me. . . . He believes in me when I don't believe in myself. He's very encouraging and he thinks I can accomplish anything."

"He has built me up in many ways, primarily with my girl things, with my hobbies, and always admiring my work and telling other people about it. He never made light of things that were important to me."

Before we move on from cherishing to honoring, let me say a word about romance. Men who wish to cherish their wives must remember that men and women approach sex and romance differently. For men, it's more of an isolated act. We are ready anytime, anywhere, and in a heartbeat! However, our wives see sex as a process. It cannot be rushed. It begins not in the bedroom, but the family room or kitchen; not with touching, but with talking; not with making love, but with making dinner; not with sexy clothes, but with folding the clothes piled high in the laundry room. Remember, for our wives, being served or pampered is the ultimate aphrodisiac. It's a medical fact: Women who feel nourished and cherished have fewer "headaches."

A SERVANT-HUSBAND HONORS

Take a look at this small section of Peter's first New Testament epistle.

You husbands in the same way, live with your wives in an understanding way, as with someone weaker, since she is a woman; and show her honor as a fellow heir of the grace of life, so that your prayers will not be hindered. (1 Peter 3:7)

I know of no other command in Scripture to which God connects a consequence like the one listed here. He says that if you don't honor your wife, the effectiveness of your prayers will diminish. This is serious business!

When you look at the meaning of the Greek word we read as "honor," you begin to understand why the Lord places such a burden of responsibility on men to extend it to their wives. The Greek word is *time* (pronounced tee-may). A noun, it signifies something you give to acknowledge value and worth. Something priceless. The idea is to esteem another person in such a way that you affirm their dignity. We are not talking about hollow words here. The command is to offer praise of which one is judged worthy. God wants our wives to be honored and praised.

How do you communicate a message like this to your wife? We got a glimpse from the older couples quoted earlier. Study the words of these fifty-year veterans of marriage and you'll see honor in action:

> You have so much potential, and I want to help you reach it.
> I want you to grow in grace and become all that God wants you to be.
> You are the pride and the joy of my life.
> I get excited about seeing you become the beautiful woman God designed you to be.

Convey messages like these every day. And don't speak with words only. Every time you honor your wife with your words, follow them up with action. Just ask a simple question: "What can I do to help?" Honor her in this way and it'll both change your life and bless your wife.

How can you show honor? Here are just a few tips, my "top ten" to get you started:

1. Praise her publicly.
2. Say "Thank you" often.
3. Open doors for her.
4. Wait on her joyfully.
5. Wait on her patiently.
6. Seek her opinion.
7. Take her advice.
8. Respect her feelings.
9. Bring her a gift.
10. Listen, listen, listen!

A SERVANT-HUSBAND UNDERSTANDS

Now, what about that admonition to "live with your wives in an understanding way"? For starters, let's dispel another misconception. The following phrase, "as with someone weaker" (read in some translations, "weaker vessel"), is not a signal of inferiority. The word *weaker* as used in this context means fragile. In other words, Peter was saying that a wife is more like fine crystal than a plastic container. Big difference, men, between Tupperware and fine crystal. At our home, we only bring out the crystal a couple of times per year—Christmas and Thanksgiving. When it's time to clear the table, those crystal goblets, a wedding gift from my uncle (an antique dealer), are *handled with care*—not because they are inferior, but because they're fragile and precious. After all the other dishes are washed, we carefully hand wash those goblets, dry them, and put them away.

By contrast, we have some plastic tumblers, and those things get anything but gentle treatment. If I'm in a hurry, I'll use one to practice my jump shot and see if I can hook it into the sink from our family room. The point, men, is to handle your wife like fine crystal, not like cheap plastic. Be sensitive to her moods, feelings, and needs. She is different by design. Recognize that. She's more fragile, delicate, and tender, often more aware of feelings and emotions than you are, and often more intuitive and interpretive of subtle nuances of communication than the average guy. And this is a good thing! Never forget: There is no hint of inferiority in that assessment.

OK, now that we're clear on that point, what did Peter have in mind here when he told us to understand our wives? We discussed at length in the last chapter the example Jesus set by becoming a human Being. He chose to spend time getting to know our "language," how we think and feel, what our needs are. What I see Peter providing here is yet another reason for men to follow this example with their wives. We're to work at understanding how they think, what their needs are, and how they most desire for us to meet those needs. Read this phrase in the King James Bible and you begin to get the idea. It says to live with your wife "according to knowledge." In the simplest terms, know your wife and know her well.

How do you get to know a person? For starters, inquire. Investigate. But this assumes that you have a skill guys are not normally famous for: *listening*. The number one complaint by women, according to one survey, is that their husbands don't listen to them. What's so weird, so tough at times, is that more often than not we feel like we *are* listening. That's why we need to pay close attention to Peter's words. We need to focus more on listening for the purpose of knowing and understanding our wives. That's more important than listening so that I can fix my wife's problems, which is the typical male approach. "Tell me what's up, what's wrong, so I can make it right." But most of the time, what a woman wants is for me to love her by listening in such a way that I hear exactly what she's saying and seek to know her better as a result.

This is a tough assignment for me. Usually when Becky comes to me with a problem, I tend to interrupt her before she's even finished and say, "You know, honey, you've got two choices here. You need to do either A or B. Pick one. Do it, and your problem will be solved." At which point she says, "But you're not listening!"

After more of these encounters than I care to recall, here's a secret I'm learning. My wife wants to know that I care more about her than about her problem. Remember that the next time you're tempted to jump in and play Superman on your wife's behalf.

Men, as you've read these words, I hope you've actually been listening to what I've said. If not, maybe you'll listen to these words from Nancy Jeffrey, a wonderful woman in our church who was married to her husband Jim just a few months short of forty-six years. "During those years," she says, "no thought was given to the idea that we would ever be apart." As of this writing, Nancy had been widowed for three years.

Now that Jim is gone, the things we should have done jump to the forefront, and regrets are numerous. I would like to challenge those of you who are young in your marriage, learn to listen attentively. It is probably the most important part of a happy marriage. Stop whatever you are doing, even though you think it is something important at the moment, and listen, with eyes looking at each other. So much can be said without even a word spoken, just by showing your mate that he or she is worth all your attention. If children are needing help at a particular time, make sure your mate will have your attention. If this isn't established as a habit now, later on in your marriage your spouse will look for someone else who will listen.

Sobering words, aren't they? Listen to Nancy, guys. Learn how to say "I love you" in the language your wife can best understand.

So how does a husband say "I love you"? He does it by caring for his wife. And how does he care for her? By sacrificing, nourishing, cherishing, honoring, and understanding her. The beauty of marriage is that love expressed like this has a profound impact on a man's wife. It actually sets in motion a circle of love that creates not only harmony but strength in marriage. Here's what this circle looks like:

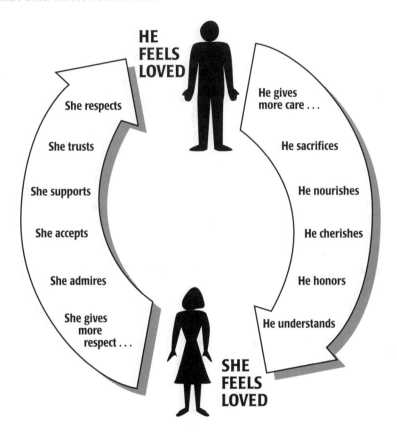

HE FEELS LOVED

She respects

She trusts

She supports

She accepts

She admires

She gives more respect . . .

He gives more care . . .

He sacrifices

He nourishes

He cherishes

He honors

He understands

SHE FEELS LOVED

In the next chapter we'll look at the left side of the circle to answer the question "How do women say 'I love you'?"

NOTE

1. *American Heritage Dictionary*, ed. William Morris (Boston: Houghton Mifflin, 1991), s.v. sacrifice.

CHAPTER FIVE

HOW DO WOMEN SAY "I LOVE YOU"?

Every guy who has ever been accused of being clueless about how women think should be particularly grateful for the heavenly advice we discovered in the previous chapter. There are ways for men to say "I love you" that address the female's primary needs. Now it's time to turn the tables and see what God says to women about loving their husbands in similarly effective ways. Before we let the guys completely off the hook, though, I have to recount a story that suggests we men still have a long way to go.

A man walking along a California beach found a bottle. He looked around and didn't see anyone, so he opened it up. A genie appeared, thanked the man for letting him out of the bottle, and said, "I am so grateful to get out of that bottle that I will grant you one wish. I'm sorry, but I can only grant one."

The man thought for a while and finally said, "I have always wanted to go to Hawaii, but I've never been able to because I can't fly. Airplanes are much too frightening for me. And on a boat, I see all that water and become claustrophobic. So I wish for a road to be built from here to Hawaii."

The genie thought for a few minutes and finally said, "No, I don't think I can do that. Just think of all the work involved.

All the pilings needed to hold up a highway . . . and how deep they would have to go to reach the bottom of the ocean. And imagine all the pavement that project would take. No, your wish is just too much to ask."

Disappointed, the man pondered the genie's reply for a while and then told him, "There is one other thing that I have always wanted. I'd like to be able to understand women. What makes them laugh and cry? Why are they temperamental? Why are they so confusing sometimes? Basically, what makes them tick?"

The genie considered the man's second request for a few moments and then said, "So, do you want two lanes or four?"

I think the message here, men, is that just because you've learned how to tell your wife your love her in terms she can understand, the lesson isn't over. You need to become a lifelong student of your wife.

However, men need not think all the homework is for them. The average wife has a lot to learn as she tackles the daunting assignment of understanding and loving the man in her life. The average woman may be more sensitive to a man's needs than he is to hers, but she faces some significant challenges. Sensitivity is one thing, but understanding goes much further. For starters, guys aren't exactly an open book when it comes time to read and understand their actions, emotions, or words. This business of building a strong relationship is, after all, much more art than science. Maybe that's why God provided a specific set of blueprints to guide women in constructing a quality love relationship with a man. Do you remember those instructions? Let's review the primary concepts found in God's Word to direct wives in loving their husbands.

As a servant-wife, she
1. Respects
2. Trusts
3. Supports
4. Accepts
5. Admires

If we're going to lay a strong foundation, ladies, this list demands your undivided attention. For that reason, we'll need to address an issue first that can quickly become a distraction if it's not clarified and resolved early in the project. The issue is found in the New Testament section of the Creator's master plan for marriage.

Wives, be subject to your own husbands, as to the Lord. (Ephesians 5:22)

As the church is subject to Christ, so also the wives ought to be to their husbands in everything. (Ephesians 5:24)

It is clear that God calls on wives to submit, to be subject to their husbands. But isn't it true that men and women are created equal? Genesis 1 and 2 affirms it. So what can this mean? If Scripture, *all Scripture,* is from God, then so is this command. The very sound of the term *submission* is enough to offend many modern couples who so want to serve as a team, pulling together to build a quality marriage. A thorough examination of the apostle Paul's concept of submission is essential to understanding God's unique blueprint to marriage, a design that transcends today's culture. As you examine God's design, you will discover that submission, properly understood, actually enhances true teamwork in marriage.

SUBMISSION: FANTASY, FACT, OR FICTION?

These verses from Ephesians don't get much attention these days. To be frank, the idea of submission is not very politically correct even in evangelical circles. But the reality is that we are wrecking marriages by ignoring it. I fear this negative attitude toward a biblical command is due to a misunderstanding of God's intent for this instruction. Perhaps the best approach for addressing the concerns associated with this text is to come at them through the back door by spelling out what submission is not. Certain words should never be used as synonyms for submission. As men and women, we must not take these distinctions lightly.

It was in a course on marriage and family at Dallas Theological Seminary that I first heard many of the concepts presented below. In that course, in the spring of 1977, my instructor and mentor, Dr. Howard Hendricks, declared, "Gentlemen, it is often necessary to blast before you can build, to deal with error before dealing in the truth." That is certainly the case when it comes to the concept of submission. If it was needed twenty-five years ago, imagine how absolutely necessary it must be today.

Biblical submission is not
- Inferiority
- Intellectual Suicide
- Without Fulfillment
- Passivity
- Silence

If we ever hope to build a solid biblical understanding of what it means to submit, we must first blast away at these common misunderstandings of submission that pervade our culture and even the church.

Submission is not inferiority. Wives aren't the only ones called upon to submit. The Scriptures are clear that even Jesus' relationship to His Father was one of submission. At the height of His anguish in the Garden of Gethsemane He prayed to God, asking to be relieved of the assignment He had been sent to Earth to fulfill. His prayer concluded, however, like this:

"Yet not My will, but Yours be done." (Luke 22:42)

This act of submission typifies Jesus' relationship with God the Father, but there is never a hint in His words that He was in a position of inferiority. "I and the Father are one," He said to the Jews assembled in the temple (John 10:30). The word *one* means one essence. Equal. This same lack of inferiority is evident just a few verses earlier in the same chapter:

"No one has taken it [my life] away from Me, but I lay it down on My own initiative. I have the authority to lay it down, and I have authority to take it up again." (John 10:18)

This same Jesus who submitted to God the Father had authority over life and death. Biblical submission does not place the one submitting in a lesser, or inferior, position. To insist that submission equals inferiority is to declare that God the Son is not equal to God the Father, a heresy condemned long ago by the church.

Submission is not intellectual suicide. Anyone who would suggest that a woman must blindly submit to her husband's leadership needs to know that to make such an assertion is just as irresponsible as suggesting that Christ calls us to come to Him by blind, unthinking faith. The opposite is the case. As large crowds were following Jesus, He didn't say, "Trust Me. Just follow Me and everything will turn out fine." Instead, He challenged them to think, perhaps more seriously than they'd ever thought before, about what they were getting themselves into.

"If anyone comes to Me, and does not hate his own father and mother and wife and children and brothers and sisters, yes, and even his own life, he cannot be My disciple. Whoever does not carry his own cross and come after Me cannot be My disciple. For which one of you, when he wants to build a tower, does not first sit down and calculate the cost to see if he has enough to complete it? Otherwise, when he has laid a foundation and is not able to finish, all who observe it begin to ridicule him, saying, 'This man began to build and was not able to finish.'" (Luke 14:26–30)

This doesn't sound like a call to put your brain in cold storage, does it? Neither is the biblical command for wives to submit to their husbands. Submission is a choice that follows serious, informed consideration. It's not acquiescence to a second-class role in the relationship. It's a choice to follow another's leadership with your brain in full gear.

Again, Jesus as the Son of God may be our strongest proof that submission has nothing to do with intellectual suicide. The Father, Son, and Holy Spirit are truly equal in Their divine omniscience. However, each has a role to play and each performs that role in perfect harmony and mutual respect. The Son submitted to the will of His Father and declared, "I have come down from heaven . . . to do . . . the will of Him who sent Me" (John 6:38). John's gospel clearly affirms that the Spirit lives to glorify the Son and see Him lifted up. But each member of the Trinity is equal in essence, fully capable, and filled with all the wisdom of the universe. It's not a matter of who is the smartest mind of heaven.

Likewise, a wife who chooses to honor God and love her husband with a submissive spirit should still be highly valued for her God-given wisdom and abilities. This wisdom may be equal to or even superior to her husband. Any man with a brain should certainly value and utilize all the gifts God gives to the woman at his side.

Submission is not without fulfillment. Nothing promises or delivers a deeper sense of satisfaction than the assurance that you're doing the will of God. Whether it's visiting widows and orphans in distress (James 1:27) or ruling a nation, like King David did, there's a matchless measure of fulfillment that accompanies every decision to do what God calls you to do. Wives who submit to their husbands according to the command in Ephesians 5:22 can expect no less.

We live in a culture that defines fulfillment as being the best that you can be. "Be all that you can be" beckons the Army recruiting poster. However, the fact is that real fulfillment is found not in the pursuit of *our* dream but *God's* dream. Fulfillment for the Christian man or woman is not being all that you can be; it's being all that God calls you to be. Pleasing God is priority one.

Supporting or encouraging your husband to take responsibility for leadership in the home should never, ever be labeled as boring or unfulfilling. Indeed, such submission is an essential part of God's design for teamwork in marriage. The wife still can, and should, play a vital role in the direction of the family . . . which leads me to my next observation on true submission.

Submission is not passivity. The verb rendered "be subject to" in Ephesians 5:22 and "be submissive to" in 1 Peter 3:1 is packed with significance. It's in the present tense, which suggests a habit pattern. It's imperative, meaning it's a command. And it's in the middle voice, meaning this is not something done *to* a woman but *by* her. She's actively involved in every aspect of marriage, including this one. In fact, there's no lack of motion implied here at all. There's plenty of action; the distinction is that it's done under another's authority.

By this point in the book, I hope it's clear that God designed women to contribute fully and significantly to every aspect of the marriage and family. Submitting to her husband as a God-ordained leader in the home should never relegate a woman to just sitting on the bench while the game rolls on. She was not designed by her Creator to be the team water girl, waiting to spring into action during time-outs and intermissions. She is more like a valued assistant coach, serving alongside the head coach for life. And if that head coach knows his job, he'll involve his prized assistant in every aspect of the game. He'll seek and follow her advice, taking full advantage of her areas of expertise. Even Jesus, as Head of the church, seeks to utilize the gifts of His followers to advance the kingdom.

A great illustration of this principle is found in the story of the champion New York Giants football teams of the late 1950s. Few would remember the name of the head coach of those great teams, but he was a winner who took his teams to the top. What was his secret? He respected the strengths of his assistants and gave them the freedom to use their expertise to their fullest. His defensive and offensive coordinators were a couple of young upstarts named Vince Lombardi and Tom Landry. Now those are two names that even a wife who hates football might recognize. At one point, the head coach, Jim Lee Howell, remarked that all he had to do was enforce curfew and keep the balls pumped up and let his two assistants handle the rest. Yet, both Lombardi and Landry knew who was ultimately responsible for the health of the team and the outcome of the game. They knew how to serve under and respect the leadership of a head coach. Fortunately, they experienced a leader who let them blossom in their own right. They would both go on to serve as head coaches known for developing the assistants who served under them. Championship-caliber husbands learn to keep their wives at their side, fully engaged in the game.

Submission is not silence. One common misconception about submission is that it condemns wives to suffer in silence when their husbands fail to lead and love as Christ leads and loves His church. No man is perfect, and disappointment, frustration, and exasperation are part of every marriage in pursuit of intimacy. Still, the clear challenge to love with a submissive spirit is given to every wife, even to those wed to men who are missing the mark. Listen to 1 Peter 3:1–2. It may not be a popular verse for new millennium marriage manuals, but it is an important part of the Creator's master plan.

In the same way, you wives, be submissive to your own husbands so that even if any of them are disobedient to the word, they may be won without a word by the behavior of their wives, as they observe your chaste and respectful behavior.

The context is 1 Peter 2:13–25, a section which lays before every Christian a lifestyle of submission. Whether men or women, we are challenged to glorify God when we face unfair or unjust treatment. Our model for responding to such suffering is Jesus, our ultimate Mentor. At the heart of the section is this description of how Jesus handled His unjust treatment at the hands of imperfect humanity.

> *For you have been called for this purpose, since Christ also suffered for you, leaving you an example for you to follow in His steps, who committed no sin, nor was any deceit found in His mouth; and while being reviled, He did not revile in return; while suffering, He uttered no threats, but kept entrusting Himself to Him who judges righteously; and He Himself bore our sins in His body on the cross, so that we might die to sin and live to righteousness; for by His wounds you were healed. For you were continually straying like sheep, but now you have returned to the Shepherd and Guardian of your souls. (1 Peter 2:21–25)*

But does this mean that women are to suffer in silent submission? Some contend that 1 Peter 3:1 calls for complete silence when it says that husbands are to be won without a word by the behavior of their wives. This is not a call to stop talking, but it is a command to stop nagging. Jesus certainly shared His heart. He spoke the truth. He shared His expectations and the expectations of His Father in heaven. But He was also willing to suffer in order to fulfill His calling. He did not revile in return. He did not utter threats. Instead, He kept entrusting Himself to the Father, the ultimate Judge, the One who would bring justice, even the score, and balance the books in the end. It freed Him to just love the sheep—those stubborn, straying sheep—even when they didn't deserve it. The result was the salvation of our souls.

In 1 Peter 3:1 God calls wives to simply imitate Jesus. To love that difficult, disobedient, even unbelieving husband without preaching to him, without demanding that he change, without threatening to leave if he doesn't shape up. But does that mean total silence? If so, we have a problem with Ephesians 4:25–27.

> *Therefore, laying aside falsehood, speak truth each one of you with his neighbor, for we are members of one another. Be angry, and yet do not sin; do not let the sun go down on your anger, and do not give the devil an opportunity.*

Honesty should never be abandoned in the name of submission. The same women in Ephesus who read "be subject to your husbands as to the Lord" had just finished hearing the apostle's strong exhortation to speak the truth and not let the sun go down on one's anger.

A side note to you men: This lesson is also relevant for you. Sometimes men, in their zeal to sacrificially love their dear wives, stuff their frustrations, hurts, or disappointments. Whether leading or following, never stop being open and honest with your spouse. Silence is as dangerous to your marital health as ignoring pain is to your physical health. When it comes to marriage, silence is never golden.

APPLYING A SERVANT-WIFE'S HEART

OK, you say, now we're clear on what submission is not. So what is it? What does it mean for a woman to submit to her husband as to the Lord? *Submission is willingly placing yourself under the leadership of another.* The Greek word commonly translated as "to be subject" or "to submit" is *hupotasso.* Its literal meaning is "to arrange under." When I hear that definition and consider the context in which the command to submit is given, images from the Psalms spring to mind:

> *Keep me as the apple of the eye;*
> *Hide me in the shadow of Your wings*
> *From the wicked who despoil me,*
> *My deadly enemies who surround me.*
> —Psalm 17:8–9

> *Let me dwell in Your tent forever;*
> *Let me take refuge in the shelter of*
> *Your wings.*
> —Psalm 61:4

This is an "as to the Lord" type of submission. The psalmist was involved in the activity. He was hiding, dwelling, taking refuge in the Lord. These are action verbs. He was willingly placing his trust in another. He chose to follow his Lord and to trust in Him. That loving, trusting relationship became a place of shelter and refuge. Similarly, the wife's decision to obey God and submit to her husband's leadership is the ultimate expression of respect and trust.

In using these psalms as an analogy, it is important that we notice also the extent of submission implied there and expressly stated in Ephesians 5:24 (emphasis added).

> *But as the church is subject to Christ, so also the wives ought to be to their husbands **in everything**.*

This is not a part-of-the-way proposition; not 30 percent, 50 percent, or 99 percent. It's 100 percent. Now would also be a good time to point out that Paul's commands to the husband demand a similarly wholehearted response. He is to love his wife, sacrifice for her, and nourish and cherish her (see chapter 4 of this book) whether she's having a bad day or good—100 percent of the time.

For those who would distort Scripture to say that a woman must obey her husband, period, be careful to note one significant exception. First Peter 3:1 challenges women to submit to their husbands even if they may be "disobedient to the word." However, this is a far cry from submitting to a guy who tells you to disobey God. Paul and the apostles put that notion to rest in Acts 5:29 when they responded to the Jewish authorities who told them to quit teaching in Jesus' name: "We must obey God rather than men." Coming under the authority of another is never a call to violate the Word of God.

It is also important that we not skip or minimize the meaning of a small word in Ephesians 5:23 because we're afraid of its implications.

> *For the husband is the head of the wife, as Christ also is the **head** of the church, He Himself being the Savior of the body.*

That word, *head,* the translation of *kephale* in Greek, is used in a variety of ways in the New Testament and other Greek writings. Its most common reference is to our physical head, that part of the body designed to hold our hair. But what does it mean when used metaphorically, as in Ephesians? Does it merely mean source, as in the headwaters of a river? This view has been recently proposed by those holding to an egalitarian approach to marriage.

After all, Eve did come from Adam, and the church does draw its life from Christ, the Savior of the body. Several articles and books have therefore surmised that Ephesians is not even discussing authority or leadership.

Or does the term *head* imply responsibility for or authority over another, as in the head of an organization? Jesus is certainly more than the mere Source of the church. He is undoubtedly the Lord of the church as well.

The evidence to support the notion that the husband as head in Ephesians refers merely to source is actually not strong. The 1985 research by Dr. Wayne Grudem surveyed 2,336 examples of how this term was used in the literature of the New Testament period. His conclusions, briefly summarized in the book *Recovering Biblical Manhood and Womanhood,* follow.

- The evidence to support the claim that *kephale* can mean source is surprisingly weak and depends on a mere two examples. Both of those come from ancient literature more than four hundred years before the time of the New Testament.
- A search of 2,336 uses of the term in a variety of ancient literatures brought to the fore no convincing examples where *kephale* meant source.
- All major New Testament lexicons specializing in the New Testament period include "authority over" as a metaphorical meaning for *kephale.*
- In forty-nine texts, *kephale* was used metaphorically to mean "a person of superior authority or rank, a ruler, or ruling part."[1]

Indeed "authority over and responsibility for" is the meaning of *kephale,* or head, in God's blueprint for marriage. Not the heavy-handed, harsh rule of the world, but the gentle, loving, sacrificial leadership of a savior. A leader who will give anything to care for his wife. One who takes his responsibility seriously, knowing he will give an account to God for the health and well-being not only of his wife, but of his entire family.

Some have even proposed that the statement in Ephesians 5:21, "Be subject to one another in the fear of Christ," negates the following command. As I stated earlier, this command is actually a consequence of being filled with God's Spirit and calls all of us, men and women alike, to exhibit a submissive spirit whether leading or following, whether husband or wife (5:22–33), whether parent or child (6:1–4), whether employee or employer (6:5–9). However, in each of these relationships someone is told to exercise loving leadership and someone is encouraged to follow. If Ephesians 5:21 removes the leadership of the husband, it would also eliminate the leadership of fathers and employers as well. Obviously, no parent would buy such an interpretation!

Others have argued that submission and headship are concepts based only in the culture of the New Testament and are not relevant to life in the twenty-first century. However, these concepts in Scripture are anchored in truths that clearly transcend any culture or time in history. Passages such as 1 Timothy 3:13–14 and 1 Corinthians 11:7–12 ground their teaching on role distinctions on (1) the purpose of Creation; (2) the order of Creation, (3) the order of the Fall, (4) the creation of women, and (5) the observation of angels. No matter how you interpret these difficult passages, one thing is crystal clear: These five facts are not culturally based. They are as relevant today as they were in the culture of the Old Testament or the New Testament.

Christ is the Head of the church and the husband is the head of the wife. Jesus is the church's Lord and Leader as well as its Source. He takes responsibility for the life and health of the church, just as the husband takes responsibility for the life and health of his wife. It is in light of this challenge for husbands to lead and love by sacrificially caring for every aspect of their dear wife's welfare that God then calls the wife to follow. She will someday answer to her Lord in heaven for how she loved and followed her leader on earth. It is a love that takes the unique form of trust, of following him as they journey together for a lifetime.

HOW A WOMAN SAYS "I LOVE YOU"

One of the most common mistakes made today in our culture is to approach marriage in a unisex sort of way. It's the counseling equivalent of the one-size-fits-all approach to your wardrobe. Sure, it may be possible to put together a closet full of clothes that could be worn equally well by me or my wife, but don't think either of us would be too excited about our fashion options! Sure, we both like lounging around in our sweats, or riding bikes in a T-shirt and biking shorts. But when we want to look our best, we are, without a doubt, different by design. What am I saying? Simply that God's directives for the husband, examined in chapter 4, are distinctively different from His mandates for our wives.

Granted, some of the principles for marital love cut both ways. A servant's heart certainly undergirds both genders' roles. Sacrificial love should never come labeled "For Men Only." A guy loves to be cherished by the woman in his life. However, those are not the issues in focus when God specifically addresses the wife. He says very little about loving your man by sacrificing, nourishing, cherishing, honoring, or understanding this guy called Husband. Why? Because God knows men. He made them—before He tackled the task of designing Woman. He knows what makes us tick. He knows what builds us up. He knows what communicates love to real men.

We've already seen that submission, as important as it is, is not the only issue. In fact, it is not even the main issue. Listen again to Ephesians 5:33.

And the wife must see to it that she respects her husband.

When God prepares to put His final touch on this classic passage on marriage, He calls the wife to respect, not submit. Why? Because respect is the real issue for men. Submission is not the end; it is only one *means* to the end. The real target in God's sights is to see wives showering their husbands with a gentle rain of respect. It is the gift that best says to a man, "I love you." Just as sacrificial love is only a tool, a means of communicating to our wives that we care, so submission is only a tool, a means of communicating respect to your husband. Even in 1 Peter 3:1–2, when wives are encouraged to be submissive to their husbands, the goal is for those husbands to be won without a word by the *respectful* behavior of their wives.

R-E-S-P-E-C-T is the issue, not only for Aretha Franklin, but for Mr. Franklin and all the men who ever married. Don't get me wrong. Women deserve and desire respect. However, our souls as men yearn for this precious gift from our wives. It means everything to us. Without it, we will shrivel up and never become the

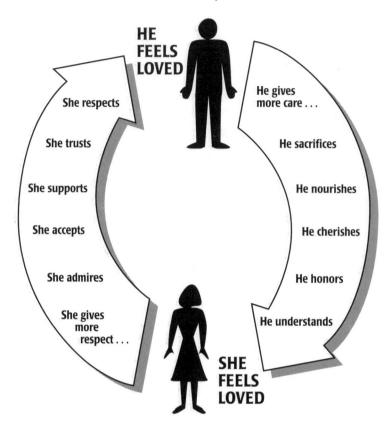

men our wives want us to be. With it, wives, we will take extra pains to care for you the way you long to be cared for.

The more I study the different places in God's Word where our Designer talks to or about the wife who pleases her God, the more I see respect at the heart of the wife's role in marriage. However, respecting your husband takes many different forms. I would highlight at least five key expressions of respectful love: *respect, trust, support, acceptance,* and *admiration.* Learn to give these five gifts to your man, and you will please your God and thrill your husband! Let's examine them one at a time, but remember that they work best in combination.

A SERVANT-WIFE RESPECTS

When you hear the word *respect,* what comes to your mind? The Greek words used in both Ephesians and 1 Peter come from the verb *phobeo* or its noun counterpart *phobos*. It's the source of our English word *phobia* and is almost always translated "to be afraid" or "to fear." When used of God it often carries the sense of reverence or awe. This reverential fear is usually reserved for God, but in Ephesians 5 and 1 Peter 3 it is expanded to include love from the wife to her husband.

Most translations, perhaps a little uncomfortable with the idea of a wife fearing or revering her husband, choose the term *respect* as the best English equivalent. *Respect* is a great term. It captures the idea of reverence while reserving that term for God alone. When I go to the dictionary to explore these two terms, *reverence* and *respect* begin to come into focus:

> **respect** (ri-spekt) *v.* 1. To feel or show esteem for, to honor. 2. To show consideration for; avoid violation of; to treat with deference. —*n.* 1. A feeling of deferential regard; honor; esteem. 2. The state of being regarded with honor or esteem. 3. A willingness to show consideration or appreciation.

> **revere** (ri-vir) *v.* 1. To regard with awe, great respect, devotion or venerate. Synonyms—revere, worship, venerate, adore, sanctify, idolize, idolatrize. These terms imply the deepest respect and esteem for a person, an object, or a deity. Revere has a sense of treasuring with profound respect—implies intense, unquestioning esteem, love, and devotion.[2]

To some degree, *respect* and *reverence* as defined above are reserved only for God. Only He is truly worthy of complete reverence and worship. Those who read the great lessons on marriage in the New Testament know that worship is the domain of God and God alone. However, they also know that respect, or reverence, is a gift that can be given to men, even imperfect men or ungodly men. First Peter 3:2 clearly calls on wives to win over their husbands by their "chaste and respectful behavior." Moreover, these guys are described in verse 1 as men who are "disobedient to the word." That is often taken to refer to husbands outside the faith, unbelievers, but that's not necessarily the case. All too often, it is the Christian who finds himself or herself with a spouse who is, dare I suggest, less than an angel. Many wives know the challenge of living with a mate who has little to no interest in spiritual things. It is to that wife that God says, "Give the gift of respect to your husband."

A very common statement that floats around this subject is "Trust can be given, but respect must be earned." Is that really true? If by respect we mean a feeling of respect or admiration, then I can agree. However, respect used in reference to marriage is not just a feeling; it's an action. It is something I can choose to give whether I feel it or not. We do this all the time. A student may not like a teacher, principal, or coach. However, he had better show those persons respect not only for who they are but for the positions they hold. A citizen may not feel a lot of respect for a particular president, judge, or policeman. However, he or she had better learn to show those figures respect. How much truer this is in a marriage. A wife's feelings of respect for her husband (or a husband's for his wife, for that matter) will grow or diminish as she gets to know him, observing his character and skills. When she feels respect for him, showing it—expressing it—will come easily. However, God isn't calling us to the easy thing, but the harder thing: showing respect whether it's deserved or not.

Does this sound familiar? I hope so. It's the same challenge God gives to husbands. The call to sacrificially love, nourish, cherish, and honor our wives isn't limited to their good days. It extends to every day after we say "I do." Ditto for the wife.

A great illustration of this unconditional respect comes to mind. Sally found herself in a marriage that was hurting and crying out for repair. The deal she thought she had made on her wedding day had slowly gone from ideal to ordeal. Her husband's number one allegiance was to his work. He owned several businesses and found little time for his wife or family at the end of the day. He was addicted to the pursuit of the prizes and toys of the earth. As he flew though life, he not only met but exceeded his goals. However, spiritual things were not even on his radar screen, and his family was little more than an occasional blip.

After a personal and business crisis, he found himself on the wrong side of the law. Next thing she knew, her husband was headed for time in a state penitentiary. Through it all, she continued to love him and show him respect. She was loyal. She avoided gossiping about her problems. She never spoke ill of her husband even in the worst of times. But perhaps her greatest show of respect came during the time he was incarcerated. Whenever their children wanted to do something special or to make a decision where a father would normally be involved, she would make the kids wait for their father to call. That way she and the kids could ask him what he thought and show him respect as the leader of their family.

What a great expression of respect for a husband and father, even while he was in prison. The good news is that God's counsel in 1 Peter 3:1–2 made an impact. The unconditional love and respect of this wife drew her husband's heart toward both her and her Savior. He accepted Christ before being incarcerated and grew tremendously during his time in prison. Since his release, he has never looked back and now embraces a new set of priorities with his Lord and his wife at the top of the list.

You see, respect is not optional; it's *essential* in a healthy marriage. What can you do if you don't have a lot of respect for your husband? Let me suggest a passage.

> *Finally, brethren, whatever is true, whatever is honorable, whatever is right, whatever is pure, whatever is lovely, whatever is of good repute, if there is any excellence and if anything worthy of praise, let your mind dwell on these things.* (Philippians 4:8)

Focus on the positive. Philippians 4:8 gives you a shopping list of reasons to appreciate, praise, honor, and esteem your man. Sure, he may have his faults, but God's advice and mine is to refuse to put your focus there. Stop and take time to identify the good instead of the bad. Tell him and others where he excels; talk about things excellent rather than things deficient. Concentrate on the actions worthy of praise, not criticism. Thank God for what is right about the man, not what is wrong. Where is he of good repute, good reputation? Every man has some areas that are honorable; talk to others about those areas. Dwell on the lovely, not the ugly; the true, not the false. Anything worthy of praise? Start praising it to anyone who will listen! I know this may seem hard at first, but trust God's manual on marriage and just do it! Focus on the positive, and see if the negatives don't begin to diminish. However, I warn you, this takes time, so commit to the positive and stay there.

Focus on the position. God calls us to respect the fact that leaders may not always be right, but they are always responsible. God will hold the husband accountable for the condition of the home, so respect that position of responsibility. When you are struggling to follow him, remember that when it comes to the final evaluation before the throne of God, the buck stops with your husband. It is not so much an issue of authority as it is an issue of accountability and responsibility. Respect that position of responsibility and his calling as the leader in your home. Permit me to paraphrase another passage—one written to call the church to respect its leaders—and apply it to our marriages.

> *Obey your leaders* (husbands) *and* (respectfully) *submit to them, for they keep watch over your souls* (and your homes) *as those who will give an account* (to God). *Let them do this* (lead out in your marriage) *with joy* (sensing your support and respect) *and not with grief* (as you nag them about their shortcomings and poor decisions), *for this* (type of disrespectful relationship) *would be unprofitable for you* (and all those in your family). (Hebrews 13:17)

Focus on the Lord. Ultimately, our calling is to the lordship of Christ, not to any human being. It is our Lord (who suffered unjustly) who is our Mentor for marriage. This is true for the husband who races to love his wife sacrificially, trying to be the first to the cross. And at times, it is true for the wife, who must give respect even when it isn't fully deserved. But if we are to be prepared to answer to God someday for our lives, we must not focus on our *husband's* worthiness, but on *Christ's* worthiness. It is our Redeemer, the Lamb of God, whom we serve. It is out of respect and worship to our Sovereign God that we give respect to those He places over us in life. This idea is so politically incorrect in today's world that it is hard for me to even type it! However, it is so thoroughly true that I dare not fail to write it. Remember that fulfillment is not about being all I want to be, but about being all God calls me to be. Living with a focus on pleasing the One who redeemed me, not with silver or gold, but with the precious blood of Christ (1 Peter 1:18–19) is always the ultimate motivation for holiness. What a difference it makes when my desire for holiness is greater than my desire for happiness. In the end, the desire for holiness is the key to real joy through all the days of my life and my marriage.

God wants us to understand that giving a husband respect and any of the other gifts in this chapter is not just about trying to please a man. It's about trying to please the One who has showered us all with more respect than we could ever deserve.

A SERVANT-WIFE TRUSTS

Trust means so much to a man. As a wife encourages and follows the leadership of her husband, that expression of trust becomes a powerful act of love. It says to him, "I believe in you." Again, do not misunderstand the point. Women certainly need to receive trust from their husbands. Everyone, man or woman, yearns to be trusted. But for men that desire is much more intense. Remember, we are different by design. Just as the woman's greater need is to feel that her husband truly cares about her, so the man's greater need is to know that he is trusted by his wife. Sure, he likes a little tender loving care, but only after he feels trusted.

Perhaps an illustration of this difference and its importance to men is in order. Suppose you, as a man, come home at night and begin to complain about your day. You're facing a real challenge. You start explaining to your wife that your associate just isn't happy and is talking of leaving the company right in the midst of a particularly tough assignment. As you're describing the size of the project, expressing some fear that you may not be able to handle it, your wife breaks in midsentence.

"Honey, I don't care what that worthless associate does. If he's not happy, let him leave. You don't need him if he's not really on your team. You can tackle this thing without him and do it in half the time, twice as well, and without all the headaches of putting up with him. Just go for it and don't look back. It'll all work out. However you decide to handle it, it will be great!" And with a quick kiss your wife returns to what she was doing.

The question is, How do you feel? If you're like me or most men I know, you feel GGGGGREAT! Why? Because the most important woman in your life just believed in you. She just affirmed you. She just reminded you that you can conquer the challenge that was staring you down. You feel loved and trusted.

Now turn the tables for a moment. Imagine that your wife has just come home at night and begins to complain about her day. She has hit a real challenge. She starts explaining to you that her associate just isn't happy and is talking of leaving the company right in the midst of a particularly tough assignment. As she's describing the size of the project, expressing some fear that she may not be able to handle it, you break in midsentence.

"Honey, I don't care what that worthless associate does. If he's not happy, let him leave. You don't need him if he's not really on your team. You can tackle this thing without him and do it in half the time, twice as well, and without all the headaches of putting up with him. Just go for it and don't look back. It'll all work out. However you decide to handle it will be great!" And with a quick kiss you return to whatever you were doing.

The question is, How does she feel? If she's like my wife or most women I know, she feels pretty ticked! Why? Because the most important man in her life just blew her off—and her problem. She's irritated because you didn't even care enough to let her finish sharing how she was feeling. She wanted to talk about the wounded relationship with the associate. She wanted to be reminded that someone—that person she married—really cares about her. Sure, she wants to know that you believe in her, but only after she hears that you really care about her. She feels loved when she is cared for. You feel loved when you are trusted. Your mistake: You didn't listen long enough, deep enough, hard enough, before offering advice. Fact is, she didn't expect advice. She expected affection, affirmation, and concern for all that she was feeling.

"But, Dale," you ask, "how do I trust when trusting isn't easy?" That's a legitimate question. Just as trust is a component of respect, so the solutions for repairing a lack of trust are similar to the solutions that apply to building up a spirit of respect. Just as in that circumstance, you need to focus on the *positive,* the *position,* and the *Lord.*

Focus on the positive. Begin by focusing on your husband's strengths. Every man has areas in which he excels. Trust comes easier when you let your mind dwell on those things. Make a list of the ten best decisions you've seen your husband make and thank God for them. If that's too many, go for five!

While counseling a young couple years ago I developed a simple technique for applying this principle. I required this young couple to each make a list of ten things they admired or respected about the other. These they were to write out on a 3 x 5 note card, and post it in an often-seen location, such as a car visor, makeup mirror, exercise machine, or even the refrigerator door (depending on which way you're wired!). What really matters is that you see it often and then pause to pray, thanking God for these attributes in your spouse. This simple daily routine can go a long way toward nurturing a sense of respect for your husband or wife. Try it!

Focus on the position. God has called the husband to lead. If that scares you, go back and read the last chapter. Remember that God's desire is not to enslave but to bless. The leadership envisioned is one modeled after Christ's sacrificial love at the Cross. It is important that the wife remember that God has called her husband to a position of responsibility and accountability for his family. Just as church leaders will someday give an account for the souls under their care, so husbands will someday stand before God and be accountable for the health and well-being of their family. A wife must trust her husband, let him lead, and encourage him to grow as a leader, for he will someday stand in the presence of God and be held accountable for the decisions and direction of his home. He may not always be right, but he is always responsible.

What if you don't agree with the direction or decision of your husband? As was said earlier, *communicate.* Share your input and observations. Every guy I know needs help as he leads. Every wise leader, like a coach, seeks to utilize the strengths of his team, especially his number one assistant. Yes, even the best of leaders blows it sometimes, but God still calls us to follow those leaders. The story of Sarah in 1 Peter 3 provides a divinely inspired challenge to every wife married to a less-than-perfect husband.

> *For in this way in former times the holy women also, who hoped in God, used to adorn themselves, being submissive to their own husbands; just as Sarah obeyed Abraham, calling him lord, and you have become her children if you do what is right without being frightened by any fear.* (1 Peter 3:5–6)

That leads me to the third secret to trusting even when the relationship is rough. When focusing on the positive and on the position still leave you struggling, always rely on the ultimate basis of security—your relationship with your God.

Focus on the Lord. It is only possible to trust your husband if your ultimate trust is in the Lord. There is no doubt that Abraham was a less-than-perfect husband. He may seem bigger than life to us—a patriarch and the father of nations, a great spiritual leader—but to Sarah he was simply Abram. Perhaps Abe for short. Sweetheart. Honey. But she also called him *lord* on several occasions. She certainly knew he was no god. In fact, she knew all about his shortcomings. She and Abraham had good days, even great days together. However, their marriage drama had its tough, frustrating, even exasperating episodes as well. Abraham, the father of faith, a preeminent hero of faith listed in Hebrews 11, sometimes stumbled. And when he fell, he put Sarah through some hard times, even placing her at risk. In Genesis 20 he even told a half-truth, claiming she was his sister (she was in reality his half sister) because he feared Abimelech the king. The story is a shameful story of a cowardly husband putting his wife in jeopardy. But it is also a great tale of God's faithfulness and protection over such a respectful woman of faith.

Again, God never expects a wife to follow a husband into sin. The highest authority and accountability in all our relationships is to our Lord and our God. But when decisions are not a matter of obeying or disobeying our God, that very God calls wives to respect and follow the lead of the man He has brought into their lives.

The only way for any woman to do this is to recognize that her hope, ultimately, is not in her husband but in her God. Sarah hoped in God, not being frightened by any fear (see 1 Peter 3:5–6). There's the secret! To trust and follow a mere man is only possible as a wife deepens her trust in God. She must believe that God will be her true Source of security and hope. It is only then that she will be able to risk trusting that wonderful but far-from-perfect Abraham in her life.

How important is trust to a man? How will such trust affect him? John Gray summarized it well.

> To trust a man is to believe that he is doing his best and that he wants the best for his partner. When a woman's reactions reveal a positive belief in her man's abilities and intentions, his first primary love need is fulfilled. Automatically he is more caring and attentive to her feelings and needs.[3]

A SERVANT-WIFE SUPPORTS

Another effective tool for loving your husband is to back him up. Every man loves to know that his wife not only believes in him and wants to see him succeed but is also willing to help make it happen. She supports him. She is proud to serve with him and be at his side. When God created woman, the first term He chose to describe her was the Hebrew word *ezer*, from a root word meaning "help" or "aid." In Genesis 2:20 the Hebrew term has been translated with phrases like "helper suitable" (NASB; "suitable helper," NIV), "help meet" (KJV, ASV), "helper comparable to him" (NKJV), "companion suitable for him" (NLT), "helper fit for him" (RSV). Get the idea? The Lord knew we guys needed a helper. And not just any kind of helper, but someone custom-made to partner with us in life.

A man feels loved when his wife says, "Wherever you go and whatever you do, I'm in. I'm with you. You can count on me. Whatever I can do to help, just call." It may be a bit corny, but men love it when women stand by their men.

A couple of tips come to mind. First, a warning is in order. There is a fine line between supporting and mothering. Respect that line. Men love to sense support, but often pull away from unsolicited assistance. If our wives jump in too often or too soon, it can make us feel like they don't believe in us or respect us. I know that doesn't make sense to most women, but trust me on this. If you act like a mother, often telling your husband how to do it or how to do it the *right* way (i.e., your preferred and superior way) he will withdraw and feel resentment. It's not that you can't give him advice. Just wait until he asks for it. Let him do it his way. It's part of his need to tackle a task and succeed.

If you just can't hold back, then at least give the advice as a suggestion, respectfully. Don't act irritated that he's approaching life or some challenge big or small from a direction different than the one you would have picked. His is normal, albeit hard-to-understand, behavior. At this point, some readers are thinking, *These guys just need to grow up and listen to their wives.* And men, there is probably some truth to that statement. As we said in chapter 4, we men do need to honor and listen to the wisdom of our wives. However, please remember, ladies, every man needs just one mother in his life. When we get married, we need a friend, a lover, a fan who believes in us, one who sticks closer than a brother, a soul mate, a helper who believes in us and loves us just the way we are. Men feel loved when they are supported.

A SERVANT-WIFE ACCEPTS

Acceptance flows from the gift of unconditional love. Like all the expressions of love on our list, acceptance is desired by all but is especially important to men. One of the most common complaints from men is "She keeps trying to change me." A wife goes into marriage with a sincere vow to love her spouse "for better or for worse, till death do us part." And she really means it. However, she also figures that long before she faces death, she will have plenty of time to perfect her beloved. After all, he was always quick to adapt to her wishes during the courtship. "Whatever you want, sweetheart," was his favorite phrase, especially right before the wedding. She figures, *I'll have plenty of time to fix him*. The problem is, trying to "fix" him begins to trigger resistance, even anger, soon after the honeymoon. Why? Because men feel loved when they sense acceptance. Acceptance is another component of respect.

Have you ever been around someone who never seems to be happy with you or your work? Such a person has plenty of good things to say, but before he leaves, or by the end of the conversation, he slips in a little criticism. He mentions one small thing that could improve what you've done. He has just a quick suggestion before he goes. His praise is always deflated with a "but." There is a word that fits perfectly here: *nagging*.

> *It is better to live in a corner of the roof*
> *Than in a house shared with a contentious woman.*
> —Proverbs 25:24

A nagging wife is as annoying as the constant dripping on a rainy day. (Proverbs 27:15 NLT)

I like the word *nagging* because it resembles the action it describes. The nagging spouse is never happy, constantly complaining. She uses the slow-drip system for reforming her man. Proverbs says her pick, pick, pick is like the drip, drip, drip of rain on a windowsill. It's not really loud. It's not even really annoying at first. But it just doesn't stop! I remember reading as a child about Chinese water torture. Well, nagging is the Chinese water torture of marriage, and it drives men crazy. It's feeling like no matter what you do, you can never make her happy. At times, nagging can have devastating consequences, as reflected in this letter I received after teaching on the subject one Sunday.

Pastor Dale,

Love is kind—service is an important part of loving. This, though, is an age of dysfunctional behaviors, and Satan certainly can find ways to convolute things. In my case, I, as a very nonassertive person, married a codependent. She knew what was best for everybody in every situation. There was only one way to wash dishes, take out the trash, fold the clothes, etc. I was not allowing her to love me unless I allowed her to dictate exactly how everything was done. From her point of view she was absolutely competent and I was absolutely incompetent. Whenever we would show any irritation she would say, "I'm only trying to be helpful!" My two sons and I have spent a lot of time in counseling related to anger not properly handled. I have gone through a year-long depression and had major surgery on my stomach, and the doctors are all quite clear that I did not rightly handle my anger at being treated as an incompetent.

But we stuck with each other. I had to be supportive, but not in the way that I was used to. Today we have a very enjoyable marriage. It was worth it to pursue loving each other through very difficult times. Just be aware that servanthood and service can be subverted and misused.

Yours in Christ,
A Member

Does this mean a wife can never mention a concern or a frustration or offer a suggestion for change to her husband? I hope by this time that you know the answer. Submission is not silence. Submission is not passivity. God wants to use our spouses to help us grow. Wives—like husbands (especially kids)—are a powerful tool for sanctification. And a man needs to know when his wife's needs or expectations are going unmet. In fact, the coming chapter on communication will demand such honesty. The key is *communicate, but don't nag.* Share your ideas, concerns, fears, or expectations, but then leave it alone. Give God a chance to work and your husband time to change. Don't bring it up time and again. And always communicate acceptance. Mix into your suggestions and criticisms a healthy dose of . . .

I love you . . .
I admire the way you . . .
I want you to know how I feel about . . . but it's not a big deal.
I do wish you would . . . but I love you just the way you are.

When the marital atmosphere is full of acceptance, approval, and affirmation, feedback will fall on receptive ears. But when a man feels he can never be good enough to please you, he will soon quit trying.

Ultimately, the secret to giving such unconditional acceptance is not found in a wife's relationship with her husband but in her relationship with God. As long as God is left out of the formula, she will think the responsibility to change her husband falls to her. She will begin to take it on herself to transform this creature from a frog into a prince. She has already kissed him, and yet he still looks, acts, and smells like a frog! She knows her dreams are not coming to life, her expectations are not being met. Something's got to change—now! So, without even realizing it, she becomes a one-person refurbishing and redecorating committee. As she does, she puts more and more pressure on her spouse to conform to her blueprint for a husband. He senses her lack of acceptance and soon loses his spirit for the marriage. She may win the battle, but she will never have the man of her dreams. Without acceptance and the respect that comes with it, he will most likely withdraw into passivity or flee to another woman who gives him that respect.

Again, does God's Word call the wife to such acceptance, even when her man is far from perfect? Listen to this:

In the same way, you wives, be submissive to your own husbands so that even if any of them are disobedient to the word, they may be won without a word by the behavior of their wives, as they observe their chaste and respectful behavior. (1 Peter 3:1–2)

Again, God had it figured out. Nagging your man never gets the result you're after. It never draws him to you or to your faith. But a respectful spirit, full of loving acceptance, can draw the unbeliever or disobedient husband like a magnet toward his wife and her faith. Acceptance is a marvelous gift of love.

One final note before leaving this topic. Part of acceptance is giving your husband the freedom to be (here it comes) *a man*. Part of the mystery of marriage is learning to accept one another as different. I'm so glad my wife is feminine. But that's not me—and she's glad. Learn to laugh at your differences. Accept the fact that men have some weird male habits. They are like spices to your marriage—they can either irritate or enhance it. I thought you might enjoy one humorous example that recently came across my desk.

Mom and Dad were watching TV when Mom said, "I'm tired, and it's getting late. I think I'll go to bed." She went to the kitchen to make sandwiches for the next day's lunches, rinsed out the popcorn bowls, took meat out of the freezer for supper the following evening, checked the cereal box levels, filled the sugar container, put spoons and bowls on the table, and set the coffeepot for brewing the next morning.

She then put some wet clothes into the dryer, put a load of clothes into the wash, ironed a shirt, and secured a loose button. She picked up the newspapers strewn on the floor, picked up the game pieces left on the table, and put the telephone book back into the drawer. She watered the plants, emptied a wastebasket, and hung up a towel to dry.

She yawned and stretched and headed for the bedroom. She stopped by the desk and wrote a note to the teacher, counted out some cash for the field trip, and pulled a textbook out from hiding under the chair.

She signed a birthday card for a friend, addressed and stamped the envelope, and wrote a quick note for the grocery store. She put both near her purse. Mom then creamed her face, put on moisturizer, brushed and flossed her teeth, and trimmed her nails.

Hubby called, "I thought you were going to bed."

"I'm on my way," she said.

She put some water into the dog's dish and put the cat outside, then made sure the doors were locked. She looked in on each of the kids and turned out a bedside lamp, hung up a shirt, threw some dirty socks into the hamper, and had a brief conversation with the one up still doing some homework. In her own room, she set the alarm, laid out clothing for the next day, straightened up the shoe rack. She added three things to her list of things to do for tomorrow.

About that time, the hubby turned off the TV and announced to no one in particular, "I'm going to bed"—and he did.

Sure, the guy in this story needs to tune in and give his poor wife a hand! But don't expect him to notice or even care about all the details of his wife's routine. Love him, accept him, and appreciate him for who he is. If you do, don't be surprised if he starts at least turning off some lights as he heads for bed. And men, if this sounds like your wife, go buy her a dozen roses for the way she manages so many of the details on the home front!

A SERVANT-WIFE ADMIRES, APPRECIATES, AND IS AFFECTIONATE

As we conclude this chapter, here's a formula for becoming a "Triple A" lover: *Admiration, appreciation,* and *affection.* Ladies, men yearn for all three. And these three are the most potent when they are delivered together. Don't ask me to explain it, but men love to know someone thinks they are special. It seems to mean even more to men than to women. Again, don't misunderstand. In the last chapter, husbands were exhorted to "cherish" their wives. Appreciation, admiration, and affection are vital components of cherishing. Our wives love to hear words such as "Thanks, honey," "You look great," "I admire the way you . . . ," and "I need you." The Word of God models this gift of praise when one smart husband declared to all, "Many daughters have done nobly, but you excel them all" (Proverbs 31:29). In today's language of love, tell the woman God brings to you that the world has a lot of great gals, but she is the most incredible lady in your life!

Women often miss the fact that even the toughest of guys yearn for the same appreciation, praise, and affection. When it comes from their wives, its impact goes up dramatically. And when it's given in the presence of friends, especially other guys, it is the sweetest of gifts! Gals, your hubby may act embarrassed. He may act like he's uncomfortable with the public praise. But trust me, down deep inside his masculine soul, he feels incredibly encouraged and loved. And he is falling in love with you all over again as every word of praise, admiration, and affection rings in his ears.

How do I know this is so effective? It is the lead strategy of the seductress in Proverbs 5. There is a reason temptation is so tempting. It appeals not only to the body but to the soul of the man. Listen to some of the strategies used against your husband by the Evil One. Then see if you can't turn them in your favor. If the Enemy can use admiration, appreciation, and affection to lure your husband, you can use this "Triple A" approach to love him.

1. *Men are turned on by praise.*

> *For the lips of an adulteress drip honey*
> *And smoother than oil is her speech.*
> —Proverbs 5:3

> *With her many persuasions she entices him;*
> *With her flattering lips she seduces him.*
> —Proverbs 7:21

These "honey lips" and "oily lips" have nothing to do with the stuff of bee hives or even physical kissing. Sure, guys love their sweets and a sweet embrace, but that's not the beginning of affection. Affection and seduction seldom start with physical touch. They begin with the sweet touch of a well-timed compliment. An esteeming, sweet word of affirmation or respect drips from "flattering lips," enticing and seducing his soul. Praise is a powerful tool that can ready a man for love.

The question is, Who is doing the praising? Is it the "other woman" or his wife? Gals, never stop admiring your husbands. Surprise him with words of praise that drip from your lips like honey. If that sounds a little outdated, remember those are the words God used to describe how to attract a man. Never stop whispering sweet words of admiration, appreciation, and respect to your husband.

2. *Men appreciate attention to physical beauty.*

> *Do not desire her beauty in your heart,*
> *Nor let her capture you with her eyelids.*
> —Proverbs 6:25

Men are drawn to the physical far more than women are. When a man's wife takes the time to make herself look good, it is an expression of love. It communicates respect, admiration, and appreciation. Men respond to those little touches because they communicate "You are worth it," "You are wanted," and "I love you." Notice that in Proverbs the seductress dressed for the man, went out of her way to meet him, and set her trap with all the fine linens, fragrant aromas, and beautiful colors at her disposal (Proverbs 7:10, 16–17). She touched and kissed him and told him how special he was (7:13–15). It is a fact that beauty goes far deeper than our bodies. "Charm is deceitful and beauty is vain, but a woman who fears the Lord, she shall be praised" (Proverbs 31:30). But that same chapter extols the fact that "her household are clothed with scarlet. She makes coverings for herself; her clothing is fine linen and purple" (vv. 21–22). In other words, she looks marvelous! It has been said that women dress for other women. There is no doubt in my mind that this is indeed the case! But just remember, as the old television commercial puts it, "Gentlemen prefer Hanes!" That maker of women's hosiery not only knows its target audience but has done its homework on us as guys as well.

By the way, men, just a hint for those of us inclined to keep a tight hold on the checkbook. If we want our wives to value their appearance and look their best, loosen up a little! Let them enjoy the mall. It's a command in Scripture! Where? Read Proverbs 31:31.

> Give her the product of her hands,
> And let her works praise her in the gates.

The blessed husband of Proverbs 31 lets his wife enjoy the fruit of her labor. She is allowed, even encouraged, to spend some of her income on herself. Whether your wife works outside the home or is a stay-at-home mom, her contribution to the family is invaluable. Encourage her to treat herself or surprise her with a gift certificate to her favorite store.

3. *Men highly value physical affection.*

> "Come let us drink our fill of love until morning;
> Let us delight ourselves with caresses."
> —Proverbs 7:18

For men, affection begins with respectful admiration. It builds with sincere appreciation. But it is the sexual relationship with his wife that best says "I love you." It is crucial for the wife to understand that most husbands value this physical act of love more highly than their wives do. Why? It's just the way God made us. We are, again, different by design.

Once again, as we open God's manual for marriage, we see that He anticipated the difference.

> *But because of immoralities, each man is to have his own wife, and each woman is to have her own husband. The husband must fulfill his duty to his wife, and likewise also the wife to her husband. The wife does not have authority over her own body, but the husband does; and likewise also the husband does not have authority over his own body, but the wife does. Stop depriving one another, except by agreement for a time, so that you may devote yourselves to prayer, and come together again so that Satan will not tempt you because of your lack of self-control.* (1 Corinthians 7:2–5)

The solution: Sex is a responsibility, not a right. It is about giving, not getting; about pleasing more than pleasure. Of course, the beauty of this mysterious act of love is that the more you give, the more you're likely to receive.

According to God's blueprint, your body belongs to your spouse. Therefore, work at saying yes to one another. Focus on giving pleasure to your husband.

Does this mean you should do whatever he wants, no matter how you feel? Not necessarily. The application of this text must keep in mind the rest of God's directives for husbands and wives, such as:

1. "[Speak] the truth in love" (Ephesians 4:15).
2. "Be angry, and yet do not sin; do not let the sun go down on your anger" (Ephesians 4:26).
3. "Do nothing from selfishness or empty conceit" (Philippians 2:3).
4. "Do not [just] look out for your own personal interests, but also for the interests of others" (Philippians 2:4).

Keep in mind that just as the wife's body is under the authority of her husband, so also the husband's body is under the authority of the wife. What great balance God provides for this significant but highly sensitive dimension of love. God, knowing our differences, calls us both to be givers, not takers, in our sexual relationship.

This may call the average husband to focus on greater patience and sensitivity and the average wife to take seriously the sexual needs of her husband. God's advice to wives is "Just say yes" as often as possible. Make your sexual relationship a priority. Don't ignore the fact that in 1 Corinthians 7:5 Paul placed your sexual relationship right after your prayer life in importance! When I first read that I did a double take. Yes, it's true. God says that if we really need to "just say no," then we should follow these four guidelines from that verse:

1. "Stop depriving one another"—don't say no often.
2. "Except by agreement"—talk about it.
3. "For a time"—make it the exception, not the rule.
4. "Come together again"—plan and keep it a priority.

4. *Men want to be wanted.*

> *Therefore I have come out to meet you,*
> *To seek your presence earnestly, and I have found you.*
> —Proverbs 7:15

Notice that the temptress in Proverbs 7 took the initiative. She pressured the man. Her pursuit was part of her seduction because she knew that being wanted builds up a man's esteem. It is another sign of respect. Men want to be wanted.

As a wife, look for opportunities to let your husband know that he's your first priority. Men deserve to be cherished, just as you do. How? Take the initiative to plan time alone. Plan a special night out without the kids and surprise him. Invite him to go to bed early, not without you but *with* you. All these gifts say to a man, "I love you." Say it now; say it often.

So once again we see that the Creator of women, men, and the mystery of marriage has delivered! God knows men, and He knows what they need if they are to feel loved. When in doubt, ladies, just think *respect*. It's the common ingredient blended into every directive for wives in Scripture. Trust him, accept him, support him, and shower him with affection. Then see if he doesn't respond. In doing so, you'll be pleasing not only your husband, but your heavenly Father as well.

WRAP UP

In chapters four and five we've seen that God's Word delivers a clear mandate to men for loving their wives. In a word, it's all about caring. Care for her. Nourish and cherish her, men, and she will deliver the respect you so long to receive. And ladies, listen to God as He closes His challenge in Ephesians 5:33 with your mandate to "see to it that you respect your husband." Trust, support, accept, and admire him and he will become the loving leader you yearn for in your heart and for your home. We as male and female really are different by design. And that's OK. In fact, it's to be celebrated! The following chart is a helpful summary as you launch out to apply what we've learned in these two critical chapters.

	Men	Women
ORIENTATION	Task	Relationship
#1 NEED	To be respected	To be cherished
WHEN STRESSED . . .	Wants to think alone	Wants to talk together
#1 COMPLAINT	"She gives too much unsolicited advice."	"He doesn't listen to me."
LOVING COMMUNICATION GIVES . . .	Trust and acceptance to him before criticism	Care and understanding to her before advice
THEREFORE . . .	Don't try to fix him!	Don't try to fix it!

It all starts with our different orientation. This doesn't mean that men can't be relational. We can and should excel in our relationships. And this certainly doesn't mean that women can't effectively focus on a task or excel as leaders in their own right. What it means is that at the core of their souls, men in general are more task oriented and women are more sensitive to the relational side of life. It has always been this way, by the design of our Creator. Therefore our number one emotional needs are different. For guys, it is to be respected; for gals, it is to be cared for and cherished. The way we process stressful situations often differs. Most guys want some time alone to escape, to think, and to process. We want advice, but only when we are ready to receive it. So ladies, avoid giving too much unsolicited advice. Lead with an abundance of trust and acceptance. And don't try to fix him.

When stressed, most of our gals want to talk it through. They want us men to just listen and listen well. Communicate how much you care before even thinking of showing how much you know! She's doesn't want you to "fix it" until she knows you care about her.

So start loving one another—but keep in mind *you are indeed different by design.*

NOTES

1. Adapted from Wayne Grudem, *Recovering Biblical Manhood and Womanhood* (Wheaton, Ill.: Crossway, 1991), 425–26.
2. *American Heritage Dictionary,* ed. William Morris (Boston: Houghton Mifflin, 1991), s.v. respect, revere.
3. John Gray, *Men Are from Mars, Women Are from Venus* (New York: Harper Collins., 1992), 135.

WHAT WE HAVE HERE IS A FAILURE TO COMMUNICATE!

If you've ever seen the movie *Cool Hand Luke,* you probably remember that comical phrase in what was an otherwise serious film. It was first uttered by the road prison's mean-spirited warden to inmate Luke (Paul Newman) after he had been captured following a second unsuccessful escape attempt. Luke's first escape had prompted a speech by the warden about the perilous position any inmate would put himself in if he were so foolish as to attempt a second breakout. Apparently Luke didn't get the message; hence the warden's memorable line: "What we have here is failure to communicate." (Near the end of the film, after his third try, Luke amended the line slightly to "What we have here is *a* failure to communicate.")

That line came to mind as I read a hilarious piece that was written by one of my favorite humorists, Dave Barry. It's in his book *Dave Barry's Complete Guide to Guys,* and it illustrates better than anything else I've read the challenges facing Martians and Venusians who try to communicate. It's titled "Tips for Women: How to Have a Relationship with a Guy." See if the first few paragraphs don't make you laugh and make a point too.

Let's say a guy named Roger is attracted to a woman named Elaine. He asks her out to a movie; she accepts; they have a pretty good time. A few nights later he asks her out to dinner, and again they enjoy themselves. They continue to see each other regularly, and after a while neither one of them is seeing anybody else.

And then one evening when they're driving home, a thought occurs to Elaine, and, without really thinking, she says it aloud: "Do you realize that, as of tonight, we've been seeing each other for exactly six months?"

And then there is silence in the car. To Elaine, it seems like a very loud silence. She thinks to herself: . . . I wonder if it bothers him that I said that. Maybe he's been feeling confined by our relationship; maybe he thinks I'm trying to push him into some kind of obligation that he doesn't want, or isn't sure of.

And Roger's thinking, . . . *Six months!*

And Elaine is thinking: But, hey, *I'm* not so sure I want this kind of relationship, either. Sometimes I wish *I* had a little more space, so I'd have time to think about whether I really want us to keep going the way we are, moving steadily toward . . . I mean, where *are* we going? . . .

And Roger is thinking: . . . so that means it was . . . let's see . . . *February* when we started going out, which was right after I had the car at the dealer's, which means . . . lemme check the odometer . . . Whoa! I am *way* overdue for an oil change here.

And Elaine is thinking: He's upset. I can see it on his face. Maybe I'm reading this completely wrong. Maybe he wants *more* from our relationship, *more* intimacy, *more* commitment; maybe he has sensed—even before *I* sensed it—that I was feeling some reservations. Yes, I bet that's it. That's why he's so reluctant to say anything about his own feelings: He's afraid of being rejected.

And Roger is thinking: And I'm gonna have them look at the transmission again. I don't care *what* those morons say, it's still not shifting right."[1]

It's funny . . . and it's true. Far more often than either one realizes, men and women who think they're communicating are getting their signals crossed, even lost in space. Where do we turn for help? Once again, the Creator's master plan promises to provide the guidance we need.

Therefore, laying aside falsehood, speak truth each one of you with his neighbor, for we are members of one another. Be angry, and yet do not sin; do not let the sun go down on your anger, and do not give the devil an opportunity. . . . Let no unwholesome word proceed from your mouth, but only such a word as is good for edification according to the need of the moment, so that it will give grace to those who hear. (Ephesians 4:25–27, 29)

ALWAYS SPEAK THE TRUTH

Knowing that because of our designed-in differences our words sometimes mean different things, speaking the truth is more important than ever. Why do you suppose Paul told the Ephesians to speak the truth with one another? I would say that one reason is because God is true. He's holy. And a surefire way Christian people can inform a watching world that they're His children is by imitating this aspect of His character. What a radically refreshing change this is in today's culture. A recent survey revealed that two-thirds of youth who go to church had lied to a parent or teacher in the preceding three months. Only slightly fewer, 59 percent, said they had lied to a peer or a good friend. And more than half, 52 percent, felt that lying is sometimes necessary.

This penchant for dishonesty is not merely a national phenomenon. According to a May 11, 1999, newspaper account, "10,000 college students in Bangladesh were expelled for plagiarism, demanding the right to cheat and attacking teachers."[2]

Paul gave another reason for speaking truth: "For we are members of one another" (Ephesians 4:25). In other words, we need this in the body of Christ. But let me ask you a question. If it is imperative that we are truthful because we're connected as a family in the body of Christ, how much more connected are we in something as sacred as the covenant of marriage? If we are to be truthful so that things work well within the larger family of God, truth telling must reign even more so within the intimacy of marriage. Without it we're like satellites out of orbit, headed for deep space with no guidance system. A commitment to telling the truth is like a compass in our lives. It keeps us alert to the way we should go in a relationship. Compromise on the truth, and before you know it you'll be flying blind.

Think of what would happen in your body, for example, if your brain began sending out false signals. If it quit telling the truth to your body. Why, you could reach your hand out to greet a new neighbor and end up slugging him in the face. You may intend to gently lift an egg and cradle it in your hand, but as the message flashes to your fingertips, your hand clamps down, crushing the egg and squirting yolk all over your face. The point is, you thought one thing, but your fingertips heard another and reacted. As a result of one simple moment of confusion in communication, you now have a big mess to clean up.

Does that sound like your marriage? When our communication circuits get crossed or confused, we end up with relational egg on our faces.

If you've ever been on crutches, you're aware of the dangers of your brain and limbs not communicating effectively. I sure was aware of that the last time I was hobbled and had to rely on crutches to get around. I was walking down a hallway on my way to a meeting when I stuck one of my crutches on a doormat. No big deal, except that the floor underneath was highly polished. So when I put my weight on that fake leg it just went whoosh, right out from under me. I kept my balance, barely. But do you know what? It showed me that there was a breakdown in honest communication there. There were no nerves running down that crutch to feel the floor, so I didn't realize until it was too late that the crutch was slipping. It's that way a lot of times in marriage. Without good communication, the relationship can start slipping and we won't even know it. And nothing breaks down communication quicker than dishonesty, a failure to speak the truth.

How committed should we be to telling the truth? Check out this text.

> He who walks with integrity, and works righteousness,
> And speaks truth in his heart. . . .
> . . . he swears to his own hurt and does not change.
> —Psalm 15:2, 4

Speaking the truth means telling the whole truth, and that's not always easy. When are we inclined to fudge on the truth? For me, it's usually when I realize that telling the whole truth is going to hurt me. Even then, God says, truth telling is the way to go. The righteous "swears to his own hurt." He tells the truth even when he knows it will work against him and possibly bring on pain. But short-term pain caused by truthfulness results in long-term gain.

Are there bounds of reason to this command? Of course. When you show up at work, for example, it's not appropriate to greet someone by saying, "Good morning. You know, that's the worst looking outfit I've seen in a long time." There are a lot of true things we don't say. How many times have you seen a newborn baby that was, well, ugly? You know what I mean. The little boy or girl just finished a marathon voyage through the birth canal. Nobody looks good after an experience like that! But you didn't go and tell the proud parents, "Congratulations. But it's too bad your baby has such an enormous snout for a nose." No one ever says that, or should ever say it. Grace demands that when we speak the truth, we do it in love. Especially with those we love the most.

What if your encounter is not with a friend's baby but with your spouse? Let's say he tried a new look and it just didn't fit. Or she slaved all day preparing a special dish that completely missed the culinary mark. In cases like that, wisdom might suggest that you withhold some truth out of love.

Like the time Becky and I were still newlyweds at seminary and on a really tight budget. She had picked out the least expensive meat at the store that day to make a casserole, and it happened to be chicken livers. One taste was all it took to realize this was not going to become a family favorite. (Actually, one whiff was warning enough to beware.) But how do I speak this truth in love without hurting my bride? I think I fumbled around and finally said something like, "Honey, I love the way you're willing to try new dishes! My mom would never do that. Same old meat and potatoes and veggies every week. Way too predictable. This is so creative!"

Of course she saw right through me and said something like, "You hate it, don't you?" At least I tried, and while my words weren't terribly wise, my effort was appropriate. Speak the truth, but keep it coated in love.

NEVER GO TO BED MAD

The next time someone suggests to you that the Bible isn't practical or realistic, that it requires people to live "perfect" lives and always keep their emotions reined in, have them read Paul's letter to the Ephesian church. "Be angry," he said in verse 26 of Ephesians 4. Those don't sound like the words of someone who's

119

expecting perpetual piety, do they? At times, Paul was saying, you'll feel anger. In fact, the Greek word *orgizō* that's translated here as "angry" is sometimes rendered "exasperated" or "frustrated." The text here is acknowledging these as normal emotions. They're not necessarily sinful, although they can be. The fact that men and women are different by design guarantees times of frustration.

How we handle those emotions when they surface is the issue. God says that when you feel angry or frustrated, deal with it. Don't put it off, and definitely don't go to bed without setting things straight. And no, your options for doing so do not include stuffing your feelings. That would violate the spirit of the apostle's admonition, "Do not sin."

Why? Because stuffed frustration always festers, producing bitterness in the process, which usually erupts later into a full-blown conflict.

As I'm writing these words, our nation is still reeling from the latest in a string of rampages that underscore the tragic effects of unresolved anger gone wild. This time it was at a high school in Littleton, Colorado. Similar stories have played out at other schools with alarming frequency. Not too long ago it was domestic violence that attracted the national spotlight when a husband was murdered by his wife, who could no longer endure his abuse in silence. And of course there was the high-profile case of the Menendez brothers' murder of their parents. Each of these incidents is an illustration of suppressed anger's potential for explosive destructiveness.

A quick review of the earliest case of sibling rivalry reminds us that this phenomenon appeared on the horizon shortly after the dawn of human history. The flash point was when Adam and Eve's firstborn, Cain, sensed that his brother Abel's offering was more pleasing to the Lord than Cain's.

> So Cain became very angry and his countenance fell. Then the Lord said to Cain, "Why are you angry? And why has your countenance fallen? If you do well, will not your countenance be lifted up? And if you do not do well, **sin** is **crouching** at the door; and its desire is for you, but you must master it." (Genesis 4:5–7, emphasis added)

We do well to notice that as Cain's anger boiled up, sin was "crouching at the door." As a result, "Cain rose up against Abel his brother and killed him" (Genesis 4:8). The same sin crouches at the door of every marriage. Each time husbands or wives ignore the divine advice to "not let the sun go down on your anger" (Ephesians 4:26), they invite an infection of the soul that has the capacity to compound over time and eventually erupt into un-bridled, ugly sin. Or, if it remains suppressed, it turns its fury in-ward, producing depression and eroding the romance of marriage. By heeding this counsel, though, we have the satisfaction of know-ing that we are not giving "the devil an opportunity" (v. 27) and the assurance that we are giving the Maker of marriage room to do His healing work in our hearts.

Some may hesitate, though, citing the call in Ephesians 4 to show "tolerance for one another in love" (v. 2). Aren't we sup-posed to just put up with some of these annoyances? Yes, we are. Tolerance and patience are great expressions of love. But if the problem is producing bitterness, if you can't get it behind you, if it is stripping the joy and laughter from your love, then you have to deal with those realities. If it's big enough to keep bugging you, then it's big enough to bring up and talk out.

BE A GIVER, NOT A TAKER

Tucked right in the middle of Paul's words of wisdom about communication is an unexpected sentence.

He who steals must steal no longer; but rather he must labor, per-forming with his own hands what is good, so that he will have something to share with one who has need. (Ephesians 4:28)

When I first studied this text, I wondered why Paul, right in the middle of talking about communication and anger and speak-ing the truth, suddenly brought thieves into the discussion. It doesn't seem to fit the passage, especially because the very next verse (v. 29) picks up the communication topic again. What I de-cided he must have been saying is that we're to let Christ radi-cally change every area of our lives. Even this one.

By switching subjects from communication to a guy who made his living stealing from other people, it's as if God is saying He wants the guy to not only quit being a thief but to become a phil-anthropist. God's saying He wants this guy—and by inference you and me—to become givers instead of takers. He wants us to work hard, but not for the purpose of satisfying our own needs. It's so that we will have something to give away to other people.

Now I realize that not many of us are kleptomaniacs, but there have been more times than I care to remember when I wanted to be a taker instead of a giver. I've gone into relationships—at work, with friends or family—thinking, *What can I get out of this? What can they do for me?* God says to come in with a different set of questions, like, "What can I do for you?" or "How can I help you?" The mandate here is to develop a giving, serving, grace-oriented spirit.

Especially in a marriage, this giving attitude creates an af-firming environment that offers daily reminders to both partners that they're not alone in the relationship. Each can count on the other's support, sometimes when they least expect it and often when they need it the most.

A great book to help you grow in this area is Gary Chapman's fine work *The Five Love Languages* (Chicago: Northfield, 1992, 1995). Common sense tells us that giving is most effective when the gifts given match those the receiver values the most. Chapman helps you identify your spouse's preferred "love language," those things you can give him or her that most convincingly convey the message "I love you." The key is to realize that we are each de-signed by our Creator with different needs, so we hear "I love you" in different ways. One husband's list might include words of af-firmation or acts of service. His wife's might be quality time, gifts, or physical touch. Once you discover and begin communicating in your spouse's love language, you'll find that the other areas of communication in your marriage will begin to strengthen as well.

Another author, Gary Smalley, says he made a real break-through in the area of communication about five years into his marriage. It came after a woman told him through tears, "I've tried for years to express what's wrong in our marriage, but I just can't seem capable to explain it. What's the use in bringing it all up again?" Here's how he explained it.

This woman had nearly given up hope of experiencing a lov-ing, healthy, and lasting relationship with her husband. Opposed to divorce, she had resigned herself to a life that offered few of the wishes and dreams she once longed for.

I had heard this kind of story before. For years, I had regularly counseled husbands and wives, spending countless hours talking to them about improving their relationships. Only now, I wasn't sitting in my counseling office. I was seated at my kitchen table. And the woman sitting across from me wasn't a counselee—she was my own wife, Norma!

That day I made a decision to understand what was happening, or not happening, in my marriage. . . .

It wasn't until we understood why males and females think and speak so differently that we began maximizing our communication.[3]

Yes, we are different by design, but those differences can work to our advantage.

LET EVERY WORD BE A BUILDER, NEVER A DESTROYER OF OTHERS

Verse 29 is a vivid illustration of the fact that when Paul issued a caution, you can always be sure it was for a significant reason.

Let no unwholesome word proceed from your mouth, but only such a word as is good for edification according to the need of the moment, so that it will give grace to those who hear. (Ephesians 4:29)

We know Paul was serious about this one because of the language he used. *Unwholesome* is the English word these translators chose for the Greek word Paul used here. I personally like the term used in the King James Version. It seems to capture Paul's intent a bit better. Let no "corrupt communication" escape your lips is how that text reads. The Greek word is *sapros,* and it's extremely graphic. "Bad" would be a socially sensitive synonym. "Rotten" or "putrid" would be more accurate ones.

Don't let your mouth become an open sewer is the idea. This word-picture registers quickly with coastal Californians. When winter hits our part of the country, instead of snow we get rain. Lots of rain. Sometimes more rain than the cities' sewer lines can handle. Consequently, after a major downpour we're not unaccustomed to hearing that there's been a sewage spill in the ocean.

Millions of gallons of effluent. As you'd expect, warnings are then issued to stay out of the ocean in the polluted area until levels of "unhealthy bacteria" return to normal.

Such is the apostle's warning. Don't let your words pollute your relationships. Instead, let every word be a builder of those you love—like pure mountain springwater rather than the dirty runoff from a storm. And the challenge here isn't to hit the mark most of the time. He said we're to let *no* word out of our mouth unless it's going to build instead of destroy. None. Nada. But how do we muster the ability to do that? I find at least four tips in the Scriptures, right in this one great verse.

Use words that are controlled. To do what God says, we need to be under the control of God's Spirit. I have to ask the question, "Am I under control?" as I get ready to speak, especially when I'm upset, which is when I tend to blow it. A good litmus test for whether you're under control is Ephesians 4:15. Are you "speaking the truth in love"? Let love guide your tongue and it'll be less likely to sabotage your mission. If you're too angry to speak the truth in love, then hold your tongue until you've cooled down.

Of course you'll only have limited success in maintaining control apart from the power of God. If you're not engaged in a growing relationship with Him, looking to His Holy Spirit for the power you need to stay cool, then restraining your words will be little more than an elusive ideal. You may keep your mouth shut a time or two, but eventually those stored-up words will explode from your lips in a burst of uncontrolled anger. Giving the Holy Spirit control of your tongue, however, is like putting a thermostat on your furnace. It can keep things from getting too hot in the house—but before that can happen you have to hook it up to the furnace and set it at the right temperature.

Use words that are constructive. Your test for this one is to ask the question, "Will what I'm about to say help or hurt?" This doesn't necessarily mean that every word you say has to be pleasant. But your words do have to be constructive. Proverbs 27:6 tells us that "faithful are the wounds of a friend." In other words, sometimes we need to confront one another, but always with the goal of being constructive. Sometimes our words of truth, spoken in love, are hurtful, but our motive must never be to hurt. See the difference? My brother is a surgeon. He hurts people all the time—and gets paid for it! But he would tell you that he hurts people only to heal them. That's how we should be too.

Use words that are considerate. The phrase "according to the need of the moment" in Ephesians 4:29 reads "according to their needs" in the *New International Version* of the Bible. Blend those two ideas together and you have a call to be considerate. "Is this the right time and place to say what needs to be said?" is the question you need to be asking.

I've shared critical thoughts with my wife Becky on occasion, but I'm extremely careful about where and how I do it. That experience I mentioned earlier with the chicken-liver casserole comes to mind. You can bet that when we have friends over or when Becky's parents come to visit, I realize that that is not the time to initiate a discussion about the infamous casserole. Why? Because words that are considerate reflect care for and sensitivity to the other person. When you're tempted to speak too quickly, just remember my adventure in dining.

Use words that are characterized by grace. In other words, ask the question, "Will I treat them with love even if they don't deserve it?" The American way is to retaliate, to get mad and get even. But grace, by definition, is giving someone the opposite of what he or she deserves. When we deserved hell, God gave us an invitation to heaven. We deserved His punishment, and He gave us His forgiveness. Then He filled us with His Spirit and chose to bless us with every spiritual blessing. That's what we're to do with our words. Don't give people what they deserve. Give them what they need. *Grace.*

We often sing about "amazing grace," but too frequently when we're finished singing we start demanding. Grace doesn't demand. Grace accepts. Grace forgives. Grace is gentle. In fact, that's another great proverb: "A gentle answer turns away wrath, but a harsh word stirs up anger" (15:1). Too often when someone has offended me, I don't think he needs a gentle answer. He needs a good verbal club over the head. Paul's counsel is, Don't do it. Be gracious instead.

If you think of your marriage as a marker board that you use to record every time you feel angry about something, then words of grace become the eraser that wipes those hurtful memories away at healthy intervals. Gracious communication helps you clean off that board and keep it from collecting too many negative, destructive, unforgiven offenses. This is the outcome of "speaking the truth in love" that we read of in Ephesians 4:15 (cf. v. 25). It's also what happened when Jesus combined grace and truth. Be honest, but with a gentle and forgiving spirit.

REPLACE ANGER WITH GRACE

Let all bitterness and wrath and anger and clamor and slander be put away from you, along with all malice. (Ephesians 4:31)

This is quite a lineup of emotions we're told to toss in the trash, isn't it? Each one for good and different reasons. All together they create an atmosphere that's charged with the potential for explosive destructiveness. Having them in your marriage is like having a leaky, malfunctioning nuclear reactor powering a spacecraft. The seeping radioactivity slowly poisons everyone on board before they even realize it. Pretty soon everyone's in bad shape. And unfortunately, the trouble is compounded by the imminent danger of an all-out explosion. So let's take a brief look at each of these words and why it's so important to eradicate them.

Bitterness. This is the emotion we hold invisibly. It's like a cancer. It eats away at our insides. The Greek word, *pikria,* conveys the notion of bad roots producing bad fruit. In some contexts it connotes extreme wickedness. This is a guaranteed marriage killer which is easily fueled by the unintended offenses which naturally arise between team members who think differently. That's why we can't afford to intentionally, knowingly make room for it in our hearts.

Wrath. This one comes from *thumos,* the Greek root for "thermos." A heat holding device. But here the idea is passion or "angry heat" according to one source, anger held inside that boils up, then eventually subsides, only to boil up again. It might even be rendered "raging," and it'll ruin a relationship in a heartbeat.

Anger. The word we read here as "anger" is slightly different from the one used in verse 26. This one, *orge,* means "violent passion" or "vengeance." If wrath is ugly heat, anger of this sort is ugly anger, and it has no place in the home.

Clamor. Rarely is the word *krauge* used in the New Testament; even less often do we read it as "clamor." In other places, it's an "uproar" or a "shout" or to "cry out with a loud voice." The sense of the word used here, though, is to shout with harsh words.

So . . . do you ever shout at people? This is an area that's on my list of regular battles I wish I didn't have to fight. What's really frustrating is that I virtually never lose my cool with friends and associates. But it's so easy in the context of the family, at home, to decide that I'll raise my voice if people aren't going to listen. Unfortunately, it gets the job done. But God says not to use that as a communication tool. Don't try to shout a response out of people. Put away clamor. Never rely on increased volume to carry the point.

Slander. Now here's a fascinating prohibition. In the King James Version it says "evil speaking" instead of slander. The Greek word, *blasphemia*, refers to speech that's injurious to another's good name. How shameful, especially when your spouse is the one you're hurting. I find more than a little irony in the fact that when it comes to husband and wife, who are "one flesh," to injure your spouse's reputation is to tarnish your own as well. How foolish.

The alternative to this laundry list of tools that should find no room in your communications toolbox is found in the very next verse.

Be kind to one another, tender-hearted, forgiving each other, just as God in Christ also has forgiven you. (Ephesians 4:32)

What a great trio—kindness, tenderness, forgiveness. All done for a reason: Because "God in Christ also has forgiven you." Is this a radical change in the way many of us communicate? It sure is. The key to pulling it off is found in the verse that precedes these two.

Do not grieve the Holy Spirit of God, by whom you were sealed for the day of redemption. (Ephesians 4:30)

Now why did the apostle Paul slip a little doctrine of the Holy Spirit into the middle of this passage? The answer to that question is our next principle.

DON'T WITHHOLD THE GRACE OF GOD FROM OTHERS

When a recipient of God's grace withholds that gift from others, he breaks the very heart of God and short-circuits the power of the Holy Spirit in his own life. So . . . if I'm going to attempt to communicate effectively with my fellow crew member on this marriage mission, I need all the help I can get. I need that divine power in my life. And being unkind or bitter or angry or unforgiving hampers that power because it grieves the Holy Spirit. To grieve the Holy Spirit is to cause the Spirit to be sorrowful, anguished, and distressed; to feel the pain of hurt; to lament or mourn. In other words . . . we break God's heart.

Why is that true? To the best of my knowledge, there is no other sin mentioned in the Bible that has this effect on our Creator, or by extension on our relationship with Him. Why is this such a big deal? I would say it's because it's an insult. It's like saying to God, "Hey, please forgive me again. I blew it today. But could you bring a legion of angels down on this person over here? And not guardian angels. Bring some revelation-type angels. Dump some bowls of wrath on that person." For us to withhold grace after we've received it in abundance, which is the only way God gives it, is an act of absolute hypocrisy. And any communication that comes in on the kind of negative channels we discussed—bitterness, wrath, anger, clamor, or slander—quickly and clearly identifies the heart of the one who sends those messages. They amount to relational mutiny. Is it any wonder the apostle used such strong language to warn us against using them?

GETTING ON THE SAME WAVELENGTH

As we consider each of the admonitions we've just covered, let's be honest. Most of us would say, "Dale, this is too radical. *Always* tell the truth. *Never* go to bed mad. Be a giver, not a taker. Choose *every* word to build up, replacing anger with grace. I don't think I can handle the assignment. I'm afraid I'll crash the ship and muff the mission." I'll grant you these are tough orders. Sometimes really tough. But I believe you can follow them—if you'll remember these three tips.

Don't look backward. Would you ever try flying a spaceship at over 18,000 miles per hour backward? No way. You look forward. How do you do that? Confess your sin if you haven't lived up to this Ephesians 4 passage. All of us have bad decisions and bad communication to confess. All of us have room to grow here. Confess your sin, claim God's radical grace for yourself, and begin looking forward. Trust Him to guide you when the going gets tough.

Go into training. Anytime astronauts are assigned to a mission, they begin training so they can perform at their best. How do you train for the assignment to communicate with a crewmate whose language seems at times so difficult to understand? I'd say start by brushing up on your communication with mission control. Study the Word of God. Pray. Engage in worship. These are the exercises that will get you in shape to become a more effective communicator, one who listens, who loves, and who can spot an opportunity to extend God's grace a light-year away.

Don't travel alone. Team up with other Christians who will encourage you in your quest to communicate biblically. Get into a Bible study with other men if you're from Mars, or women if Venus is your home planet. Or gather with other couples. Either way, you need people around you who will be honest with you. I need people who will say, "Hey, Dale, you were way too harsh in your tone of voice when you spoke to Becky then."

Is there anyone in your life who will help you like that, so that when you stray they can help you get back on course? And yes, you will lose your bearings on occasion. You will wander from the way you should be going. That's where God's grace kicks in to help . . . when your power is failing . . . and provides that navigational correction you need.

By the power of the Holy Spirit, you can be like Jesus in your communication with the person you love the most, expressing both grace and truth in every word.

NOTES

1. Dave Barry, *Dave Barry's Complete Guide to Guys* (New York: Fawcett Columbine, 1995), 59–61.

2. *The Orange County Register,* 11 May 1999, p. 3.

3. Gary Smalley and John Trent, *The Language of Love* (Pomona, Calif.: Focus on the Family, 1988), 29–30.

CHAPTER SEVEN

GRACE: FORGIVENESS OFFERED, FORGIVENESS RECEIVED

After God created men and women, one of their earliest acts as Earth's first human inhabitants was to mess up. Huge. Think about it. They were set for eternity. The only perfect man to ever live on the planet (until Jesus, of course) is settled into the perfect job tending the coolest zoological park ever created. All of God's creation under his care, but no cages, no messes to clean up, and no crowds or long lines at the best attractions. Beachfront property was so cheap it might as well have been, well, free! And God drops by for fellowship every day.

But as we learned earlier, this perfect scene needed one final touch from the Creator—Eve, the perfect wife. So God pulled off the perfect approach to love, dating, and courtship . . . take a nap, wake up sore in the rib cage, and meet the wife of your dreams! The perfect start to a beautiful love story. But rather than living happily ever after, we read at the end of only the third chapter of Genesis that Adam and Eve were "driven" from the Garden of Eden. God ran them out of Paradise! Eve took a taste of sin, Adam followed suit, and the blaming and shaming started.

Now, if the story ended there, we'd all be in permanent trouble. The good news, literally, is that the entire rest of God's recorded story, all 1,185 chapters, is an account of His redemption plan. His plan to put these two lives, and the lives of countless couples since, back together. And at the heart of this relational repair job is God's specialty, forgiveness. It's about forgiveness—why we need it, how God extends it, what happens when we receive it, and how we're to extend it to others.

Marriage is at times the most important and most difficult relationship in which to practice biblical forgiveness. It's the most important because it is this relationship of a man and a woman that serves as a metaphor for the redemptive relationship between Jesus Christ and His church. It's difficult because, despite the many differences between men and women, we share the dangerous tendency to shirk responsibility and blame the other person. This weakness, which is so glaring in the biblical account of what we call the Fall, or humanity's descent into sin and separation from God, makes an already tough task all the more challenging. Look at the Genesis record of Adam and Eve's responses when God confronted them with their disobedience.

They heard the sound of the Lord God walking in the garden in the cool of the day, and the man and his wife hid themselves from the presence of the Lord God among the trees of the garden. Then the Lord God called to the man, and said to him, "Where are you?" He said, "I heard the sound of You in the garden, and I was afraid because I was naked; so I hid myself." And He said, "Who told you that you were naked? Have you eaten from the tree of which I commanded you not to eat?" The man said, "The woman whom You gave to be with me, she gave me from the tree, and I ate." Then the Lord God said to the woman, "What is this you have done?" And the woman said, "The serpent deceived me, and I ate." (Genesis 3:8–13)

There's no fessing up here. No taking the higher, harder road of truth telling. It's finger pointing from the get-go for these two. Now, imagine with me, if you will, the scenario outside the garden just moments after God had exiled this couple from Eden.

ADAM: "You know, we wouldn't be in this mess if you hadn't listened to that stupid serpent."

EVE: "Yeah, well it's not like God didn't give you a brain of your own when He put you together. Maybe it wasn't such a great idea to take *that* particular piece of fruit, but if you had exercised a little more leadership and warned me, the whole thing probably would never have happened."

ADAM: "Oh, I get it. Now *I'm* the bad guy. I hate it when you do that."

EVE: "Do what?"

ADAM: "Lay a guilt trip on me when you mess up."

EVE: "So *you* didn't mess up? Aren't those apple seeds stuck in your teeth there?"

ADAM: "Very funny. You know what? I've had it. I'll be over there looking for some ground to cultivate. Why don't you come find me when you're ready to apologize."

EVE: "Apologize! It'll be a cold day outside the Garden of Eden before I apologize for a mistake *you* made. How about if you apologize for taking the worm's way out instead of coming to my defense back there in the garden? I'm not cultivating one square centimeter of ground until you say you're sorry. So just go find your own tree to sleep under until you grow up!"

If this is even remotely how the dialogue went, it seems these two got things worked out pretty quickly, because the very next chapter begins, "Now the man had relations with his wife Eve, and she conceived and gave birth to Cain" (Genesis 4:1). We have no idea how much time elapsed between these two chapters. It could have been an hour, a day, or a decade! One thing's for sure; if it had been my wife Becky and me, something would have had to happen between the end of Genesis 3 and the start of chapter 4. That something is called *forgiveness*. So at that point I'd say the die was already cast. Knowing how to forgive was going to be part of the job description for both partners in a marriage if they intended to have a healthy union and if they hoped to bring the joy back into their new home. They would have to learn the art of giving and receiving grace, and so do we.

Before we can talk about forgiveness, though, we need to talk about context. What should characterize a relationship in which forgiveness flows freely? Forgiving is a tough assignment under the best of circumstances. It's excruciatingly difficult in a relationship where little groundwork has been done to create enough wobble room to allow for offenses, mistakes, and disappointments, let alone apologies, repentance, and healing. So let's see what the Maker of heaven and earth has to say about this delicate challenge.

GRACE RELATIONSHIPS: WHAT ARE THEY?

The end of Ephesians 4, our focus in the last chapter, should be a great relief to anyone who needs to be reminded that God understands the realities and struggles that accompany living by faith in a flesh-and-bones body. First, the text acknowledges emotions that we all battle—bitterness, wrath, and anger—and the kind of behavior they trigger: clamor and slander. But we also learn that God has emotions too. It says in verse 30 that we're not to "grieve the Holy Spirit of God." I don't know about you, but I'm inclined to keep working at this life of faith when I learn that it's not sinful to have strong emotions. God has kids just like a lot of us do, and when His kids are ripping each other apart or refusing to forgive each other, it breaks His heart. If God can grieve, it must be OK for me to grieve too. And there's a reason these wounded relationships break God's heart. It grieves Him to think that His children, the offspring of the God of grace, refuse to *give* the one gift He lavishes on all—forgiveness. God understands our hurts because we hurt Him daily. We fall short of His expectations. We make promises we do not keep. Our sin truly causes God to grieve. But He, the injured One, the innocent and holy One, still holds out forgiveness. Believe me, Jesus knows what you are going through when you are faced with the need to forgive.

What I find especially encouraging, though, is that God doesn't just empathize with our struggle. He gives us a remedy for the pain we inflict with the hurtful words and actions that erupt when we lose control of our emotions. That remedy is forgiveness, and grace relationships are the environment in which it can be applied.

Let all bitterness and wrath and anger and clamor and slander be put away from you, along with all malice. Be kind to one another, tender-hearted, forgiving each other, just as God in Christ also has forgiven you. (Ephesians 4:31–32)

We've all endured offenses from people. Often we feel justified in lashing out at them. We feel angry—and rightfully so. At least that's what we tell ourselves. After all, isn't that how justice is done? It sure feels like the best way to respond. At least it feels good to vent! But this text suggests an alternative response. It says that we're to "put away" those reactions. We're to hold back our bitterness and forgive, "just as God in Christ also has forgiven you." Do you know what the Bible calls that kind of unexpected response? Mercy. Just as the world was shocked when Christ extended mercy on Calvary, so a merciful reaction to a wrong suffered will raise eyebrows today.

I saw this happen with a couple I counseled who faced unexpected pressure from their friends when they chose to forgive rather than flee. They had both allowed the flame of their romance to burn down way too low. I wish there were a softer way to say it, but the husband was a womanizer. His wife suspected affairs. So when she met a sweet executive who treated her tenderly and complimented her often, she had an affair. Not long after that, she accepted Jesus' offer of forgiveness and became a Christian. A few months later her husband did as well. Now what? Both of them had friends saying "Leave him!" and "Leave her!" Fortunately, they listened to their new Friend, Jesus, and went to work at forgiving each other and restoring their relationship. Today the flame of their love is once again burning brightly.

Since marriage is the milieu in which we're looking to apply this biblical counsel, what can we expect mercy to accomplish there? First, all kinds of positive options become available when you choose to respond mercifully—anger can be diffused, dignity can be preserved, gratitude can grow, and peace can be restored. Conversely, a host of other options surface if you receive mercy when you know you deserve much worse. These options include the possibilities that joy can be retrieved, confidence can be rebuilt, and trust can find a fresh footing. Not a bad return on your investment, huh?

Making room for mercy is only half of the equation, though, for developing a grace relationship. It's not only a matter of withholding the hellfire that seems like such an appropriate wage for wrongs suffered, of not giving what someone deserves. Paul suggested that we go a step further, that we repay callousness with kindness, and ill treatment with tenderheartedness. This kind of response is grace personified, translated out of theology and into life. Mercy and grace are essentials for every marriage, whether in crisis or just for routine maintenance and care. But note the difference:

Mercy • *not giving* someone what they *deserve*

Grace • *giving* someone what they do *not deserve*

We all like being let off the hook. That's *mercy*. And every husband or wife who has ever dropped the ball appreciates it. But grace is so much sweeter and rejuvenating to our marriage. It doesn't just hold back the wrath; it delivers the gift instead. That's *grace*. It's a subtle difference. It's like the other side of the coin. Mercy on one side, grace on the other. It's a coin every marriage needs, because no matter how you toss it, you both win. Every time.

What do mercy and grace in action look like? The illustration Paul provided is Christ at Calvary. It's embedded in the verse that immediately follows every child's first memory verse: "For God did not send the Son into the world to judge the world, but that the world might be saved through Him" (John 3:17). Here you have the Son of God humiliated, enduring mankind's most gruesome, torturously slow form of capital punishment, without cause. For that heinous offense, and every other one before and since, we deserved judgment, but God withheld it. That's mercy. If that wasn't amazing enough, He suspended our death sentence and offered salvation instead. And you *know* we didn't deserve it. That's grace. Mercy put us back in neutral with God. No longer His enemy. But grace went beyond fixing the enmity; it declared us to be *friends* of God (John 15:14). Better yet, *children* of God. No, even better yet, *coheirs* with Christ with an inheritance:

> To obtain an inheritance which is imperishable and undefiled and will not fade away, reserved in heaven for you, who are protected by the power of God through faith for a salvation ready to be revealed in the last time. (1 Peter 1:4–5)

Now that's *really* grace! How about mercy and grace on display in marriage? Try out these scenarios:

• I come home forty-five minutes late for dinner after promising that I'd be on time, and Becky not only withholds a well-deserved reprimand but gives me a hug and says these things happen and she understands.

- I forget to make special plans for our anniversary and walk in the house with only a card, a kiss, and an apology. Becky downplays my faux pas, suggests that we go out for a bite to eat, and surprises me with a gift she picked up six weeks ago.

- I'm doing some work in the study and Becky pokes her head in to find out when I'll be ready to go for that bike ride we've planned. I snap an impatient, "When I'm finished here," in reply, and she responds with a friendly, "OK, just let me know when you're ready," and hands me a glass of iced tea besides.

Granted, these are fairly mild infractions, but you get the point. We can all think of extreme examples too, like the woman who resists the desire to divorce when her now repentant husband has been unfaithful. Whether it's large issues or small, the question is the same. Does your marriage operate in an environment where mercy and grace allow room for failure and forgiveness?

GOD'S FORGIVENESS: A MODEL FOR GIVING GRACE

We find a great model for both giving and receiving forgiveness in the New Testament letter to the Hebrews.

"And their sins and their lawless deeds I will remember no more." Now where there is forgiveness of these things, there is no longer any offering for sin.
Therefore, brethren, since we have confidence to enter the holy place by the blood of Jesus, by a new and living way which He inaugurated for us through the veil, that is, His flesh, and since we have a great priest over the house of God, let us draw near with a sincere heart in full assurance of faith, having our hearts sprinkled clean from an evil conscience and our bodies washed with pure water. (Hebrews 10:17–22)

This text hints at four aspects of grace giving. Let's look at each one.

Grace chooses not to get even. The heart of forgiveness is when I resist the temptation to even the score and choose to forgive instead. This is true of God and how He forgives us. "Their sins and their lawless deeds I will remember no more" is what the text says (Hebrews 10:17). Just as God says He won't punish us for what we've done, we follow His example when we choose not to get revenge.

We find the same message in Paul's letter to the Romans when he said, "Never pay back evil for evil to anyone" (Romans 12:17). What a great verse. This releasing of the right to get even is at the heart of forgiveness between you and me, between me and my wife, between you and your spouse. If I have a forgiving heart, I never pay back evil for evil to anyone. I freely give up any intention of getting even.

It helps if I recognize that this isn't easy. It goes against my innate desire for justice. Justice is giving someone what they deserve. What's wrong with that! After all, isn't God just? The Judge of the universe loves justice, doesn't He? But marriages aren't built on justice. Trying to always even the score will put your marriage into a downward spiral of tit for tat, of "If you, then I . . . ," or a series of "so, take thats." These things aren't just hurtful; they're *lethal!* Grace breaks the cycle of revenge and triggers a process of repair. It replaces pain with pleasure, cruelty with kindness, cutting words with compliments. Grace has the power to truly turn things around. And it begins by surrendering my suppressed right to get even.

I saw this kind of response once after a friend's home was robbed and his car stolen. The thief was apprehended and my friend and his wife were told to appear in court or else the offender would go free. They showed up intent on seeing this guy pay for his crime, which should have included a grand theft auto charge. Rather than take his chances with a trial, the guy plea-bargained a reduced charge that netted him a five-month jail sentence. My friend was initially infuriated by the invasion of his family's privacy and the reduced charge, but later began asking himself how he could demonstrate forgiveness instead. He decided to visit the thief in jail and express his forgiveness directly, and found that simply deciding to make that visit lifted a load of vengeance off his own heart. (As it turned out, it's good he experienced the benefit of forgiving that way, because when he called to see about making the jail visit, he learned that the guy's sentence had been reduced to only five weeks due to overcrowding in the jail!)

Grace chooses not to keep score. "I will remember no more" (Hebrews 10:17) is what God says of our sinful ways. What makes this statement so significant is that it's a choice to forget our offenses, to put them out of His mind. Similarly, when we say we forgive and forget, we're expressing a decision to let go of the offense and a refusal to hold it against the offender anymore. We find the same sentiment expressed in Paul's first letter to the Corinthian church.

> *Love . . . does not take into account a wrong suffered.* (1 Corinthians 13:5)

In the original Greek text, the words *take into account* here literally mean to keep a ledger. This is accounting terminology, and its message is clear. Forgiving means choosing to forget, to not bring the offense up again. Lewis Smedes addressed this mandate in his book *Forgive and Forget.*

> When you forgive someone for hurting you, you perform spiritual surgery inside your soul; you cut away the wrong that was done to you. . . . Detach that person from the hurt and let it go, the way a child opens his hands and lets a trapped butterfly go free.[1]

What a great picture of forgiveness. With men and women, forgiveness of this sort is a great gift of love. You can just imagine the impact such a response would have in the midst of an argument. Instead of dredging up old stuff and triggering resentment, God says to bury the hatchet and refuse to mark the grave.

It's not that we literally forget past offenses. That's impossible. God in His omniscience doesn't literally forget my sin. No serious theologian would imagine God, as I meet Him face-to-face and express my sorrow for the times I have hurt Him, saying, "Now, Dale, your memory must be better than Mine (scratching His head). I just can't recall any of those sins you're talking about." No, God won't lose His memory, but He will choose to give up His right to punish me. And He will not choose to present me with a ledger listing all the debts I must repay before enjoying the fruits of heaven. That's grace in action.

In our marriages, we have that same choice every day, from the moment we say, "I do." I don't just bury the hatchet; I choose to not even mark the grave, because I'm never going back.

Grace chooses not to be demanding. When the text says, "Now where there is forgiveness of these things, there is no longer any offering for sin" (Hebrews 10:18), God is letting us off the hook. He's telling us that grace is unconditional. Our forgiveness is not like a down payment with future installments due. God is not saying, "I accept you now, but later on I want you to go offer some things to cover your sins." All of our sin has already been covered at the Cross. We find the heart of this unconditional grace in Paul's letter to the Roman Christians:

> But if it is by grace, it is no longer on the basis of works, otherwise grace is no longer grace. (Romans 11:6)

Notice the definition we're being given here. The Bible is saying that you cannot claim to give grace to someone if you insist on attaching phrases like "I will forgive you if . . . ," or, "I will forgive you when . . ." Add demands such as these and you're no longer offering grace. You're proposing a deal. You're requiring a wage or some kind of payment before you will act, and grace will have no part of such an arrangement. And neither should you if you're hoping to see forgiveness do its divine work in your marriage. You have to stop demanding when you've been wronged by your wife or husband.

Is that a tough assignment? You bet it is, because at times you feel justified in attaching conditions. You want to be clear about the consequences if no repentance occurs and nothing changes. Let me offer one clarification. I'm not saying that you can't be honest. As you'll see, honesty is not even optional; it is demanded. But be honest and express your hurts and expectations (God certainly does!) in an atmosphere of grace. God doesn't threaten to throw us out of the family, but He does communicate His disappointments with the past and His expectations for our relationship in the future. And He motivates us to respond by engulfing all of this honest communication in grace and unconditional love. Your husband, your wife, may be different by design, but we all need that kind of out-of-this-world grace.

Grace chooses not to withhold love. After God said in the tenth chapter of Hebrews that "their sins and their lawless deeds I will remember no more" (v. 17), He followed this promise with an invitation to reconciliation:

Therefore, brethren, since we have confidence to enter the holy place by the blood of Jesus, . . . let us draw near with a sincere heart in full assurance of faith. (Hebrews 10:19, 22)

God is saying that not only does He want to forgive you but He also wants to encourage you to trust His forgiveness and draw near to Him so that your relationship can get back on track. Apply this approach in your marriage and your response to an offense is to invite your spouse back into a reconciled love relationship. We see this spirit of reconciliation expressed concisely in Paul's letter to the Romans.

*If possible, so far as it depends on you, be at peace with all men. . . . Do not be overcome by evil, but overcome evil **with good**.* (Romans 12:18, 21, emphasis added)

The signal here is clear. You, the offended one, are to be taking the initiative and inviting repair, renewal, and reconciliation. Rather than withholding love, you extend it, selflessly. Lewis Smedes put it this way (emphasis added):

You will know that forgiveness has begun *when you recall those who hurt you and feel the power to wish them well.*[2]

As you consider an area or an incident in your marriage that has required forgiveness, and you feel you've found the grace to extend that forgiveness, it's healthy to ask yourself, "Do I wish my husband well?" "Do I wish my wife well?" If the answer is yes, then you've exercised grace. You've forgiven and forgotten, unconditionally and in the healthiest sense of those terms, and you've invited reconciliation. That's exactly how God forgives us when we sin against Him, and it's our model for forgiving each other as well.

While this brand of grace-guided forgiveness can be tough to pull off, you'll also find that it's able to restore relationships that have endured some of the toughest attacks. Like Janet and Barry's marriage.

After nearly twenty years together, this couple had worked through many of the issues that followed them into their relationship. Married as non-Christians, they had come to faith and had been growing steadily in their daily walk with Jesus Christ. Through Barry's consistent love for her, Janet had overcome much of the abuse of her past and learned to trust again. Thanks to her support of him, Barry had grown confident in his roles as husband and father. Their children benefited from the lessons their parents had learned and were raised in a home where expectations were spelled out, praise was freely given, and personal struggles were tackled together. Communication was open and love was expressed.

Then one day, when the children were all teenagers, the youngest noticed something mysterious on the family's home computer. A quick investigation turned up the unthinkable. Someone in the house was hitting an Internet pornography site. His older brother? An uncomfortable confrontation drew not only an immediate denial but a revelation too distasteful to fathom. Dad? Yes, Barry had allowed himself to be lured into Internet porn. It's as available as candy at the corner market and Barry had taken the bait when he stumbled upon one of the filthy sites. Thanks to the same family dynamic that had allowed brother to confront brother, they both now stood before their dad, trembling, asking what they knew to be true, yet hoping it wasn't so.

Barry's initial evasiveness only intensified their anguish, and by the time he admitted his sin, Janet was reduced to emotional rubble. This man whom God had used to teach her to trust had violated that sacred bond. For a lewd image on a computer screen? Questions crushed her, then clawed at her broken heart as answers remained far beyond her reach. How could he? What was wrong with her? Does he realize what he's done to the children? To our family? The violation was akin to adultery. When friends arrived after Barry called to confess and ask for help, they found Janet spent with weeping and the children either inconsolable, in shock, or both.

The next few days were spent grieving. Anger attacked by the hour. But despite that initial onslaught, Janet fought her desire to run away and chose instead to stay and fight for her marriage. To forgive her husband. To love him enough to gradually forget her pain and remember his track record of fidelity . . . to give him time to find out what caused such a grievous lapse in judgment . . . to wait and pray for her feelings of love to return. Janet issued no conditions, expressed only hope. She chose to initiate a process of reconciliation even though she felt more like filing for divorce. And the last time we were together, Janet and Barry were smiling again, holding hands, expecting God to continue the process of healing that His grace was working in their hearts and in their home.

GOD'S FORGIVENESS:
A MODEL FOR RECEIVING GRACE

Sometimes it seems the only lesson in life that's harder than learning how to forgive is learning how to receive forgiveness. Much has been said about looking to Jesus as our role model for offering grace, but reconciliation can be short-circuited by a failure on the other end, the receiving end. The "guilty" partner is unwilling to receive or sees no need to receive forgiveness. God offers forgiveness, but for us to be restored and reconciled, for the relationship to be healed, the guilty party must have the right spirit. The Bible calls it *repentance.* Fortunately, God gives us a model. We're to receive forgiveness the same way He tells us to receive salvation.

> *Let us draw near with a sincere heart in full assurance of faith, having our hearts sprinkled clean from an evil conscience and our bodies washed with pure water.* (Hebrews 10:22)

If you've offended your spouse and are seeking forgiveness, this verse and those immediately following it are your road map to reconciliation. Here you have a guide for authentic restoration. It starts with *attitude.*

- A Humble Heart,
  seeking mercy, not grace.
- A Repentant Heart,
  eager to change.
- A Committed Heart,
  reaffirming your vows.
- A Loving Heart,
  ready to work.

Come with a humble heart, seeking mercy, not grace. If I've wronged my wife, I deserve nothing from her. Certainly not grace. The only appropriate way to approach her is the way I approach God when I'm seeking a restored relationship with Him. "God, be merciful to me, a sinner!" (see Luke 18:13). I should seek only mercy, which we've already learned is to have the one I've offended not give me what I deserve. "Be merciful to me, a husband" says I'm bringing no expectations to the table. What I receive is entirely Becky's call. I demand nothing, but humbly seek mercy.

After all, think of the alternative. Let's say I lose my temper big time with Becky. I yell at her, put her down, then come to her and say, "You know, sweetheart, I'm sorry. Will you forgive me?" And then, before she can even respond, I add, "You know, honey, you owe me not only mercy, but grace. So since I've apologized, take the kids to a movie and then come home and fix me my favorite shrimp and steak while I put on some soft music—and we'll just enjoy a nice romantic evening together."

For Becky to give me mercy is one thing. For me to expect all the blessings of grace to be *instantly* restored to our relationship is quite a different matter. That would be grace, and God wants her to grant it. But I would have no right to expect it, much less request it, and certainly not demand it.

Come with a repentant heart, eager to change. So I come seeking only mercy. Can I at least hope for grace? Sure you can, but the text suggests that it rightfully hinges on your response to your own sinfulness. As the offender, I see the phrase "having our hearts sprinkled clean from an evil conscience and our bodies washed with pure water" (Hebrews 10:22) as a clear metaphor for cleaning up my act. I don't come simply appealing to my wife's merciful nature. I come saying I'm aware of my error and am willing to walk away from it. To change my ways. And as Lewis Smedes said, I need to be willing to solicit my wife's help in figuring out what kind of changes need to take place. "The price of their ticket into your life is an open ear; an open mouth gets them only halfway."[3]

Isn't that good? If I come to Becky with an open mouth, asking for her forgiveness, I also need to bring an open ear, ready to hear how I hurt her. I need to let her tell me what needs to change to improve our relationship, which leads to our next point.

Come with a committed heart, reaffirming your vows. Where do I get this idea? Look at the next verse of Hebrews 10.

Let us hold fast the confession of our hope without wavering, for He who promised is faithful. (v. 23)

When I return to God, I lay hold of my confession of faith. My covenant with Him. Again, this is a great model. When I come to my spouse requesting forgiveness, I need to say, "By the way, I want you to know that I'm committed to our relationship." I need to assure her that my misbehavior is a lapse in judgment, not a signal that I'm bailing on my commitment. After enduring angry words or unkind remarks or extended insensitivity or worse, it may not seem logical, but it would be perfectly normal for a husband or wife to wonder whether those offenses revealed cracks in the foundation of the relationship. You need to squelch that reaction quickly and clearly. Assure your spouse of your unconditional, lifelong commitment to your marriage.

This is crucial to restoration when the relationship has been wounded by infidelity. Even if you've confessed and repented and are trusting that your actions are communicating this message, say it again anyway. Your spouse needs you to look deeply into her eyes or his eyes and express the reality of your contrition and depth of your commitment.

Come with a loving heart, ready to work at the relationship. When I come back to the church or back to Christ, here's the challenge in Hebrews.

And let us consider how to stimulate one another to love and good deeds, not forsaking our own assembling together, as is the habit of some, but encouraging one another; and all the more as you see the day drawing near. (Hebrews 10:24–25)

Again, what a great model for restoring your most precious but injured relationship. Just as you strengthen your ties with the church family by "not forsaking . . . assembling together," you need to make a similar recommitment to let your spouse know you mean business when it comes to your marriage. If I want to communicate this message to Becky, it might sound like this: "Honey, let's get our schedules back under control. Let's spend more time together. Help me to be the kind of husband I need to be." That's what it means to work on the relationship.

Whether you're on the giving end of grace or the one receiving it, you're engaged in one of life's most arduous assignments. When we've been wronged, forgiveness runs absolutely counter to our nature. It's like the dentist telling you to relax as he's about to drill a cavity into your tooth. Your natural response is to grip the arms of the chair and hang on for dear life. And when we've injured the one we love, a battle rages within as we try to rationalize our behavior and minimize our responsibility. The idea of coming clean and throwing ourselves at the mercy of the one we've offended, expecting nothing in return, flies in the face of our senses of pride and self-preservation. But according to the Creator's flight plan, it's the only way to go.

HANDLING THE ABUSES OF GRACE

Forgiveness is not an easy assignment. No getting around it. I'm reminded of this reality every time I read the account of Jesus' final anguished hours before His betrayal, arrest, and crucifixion. "My soul is deeply grieved, to the point of death," He told His disciples. "Remain here and keep watch with Me." Then "He went a little beyond them, and fell on His face and prayed" (Matthew 26:38–39).

Have you ever fallen on your face as you started to pray? Because few of us have, I doubt that we've given much thought to the kind of emotional tug-of-war that would prompt such prostration. Forgiveness was Jesus' mission here. Land on Planet Earth; live among her sorry, sinful lot for thirty-three years; allow the inhabitants to brutalize You for a while; and then, "while [they] were yet sinners" (Romans 5:8), give up Your life for them. With an assignment like that, is it any wonder that Jesus had second thoughts as His face hovered over the dark, dank Gethsemane ground? "My Father, if it is possible, let this cup pass from Me" (Matthew 26:39) seems like a perfectly reasonable request under the circumstances, don't you think? What's most remarkable is that, upon quick reflection, Jesus amended His request and abdicated to the authority of His Father: "Yet not as I will, but as You will."

Forgiving another person is difficult under the best of circumstances. Jesus' words allow us to acknowledge that the assignment becomes terribly more difficult when there's a high probability the forgiveness you're extending will be abused. I think that Mrs. Washington would agree.

According to Prison Fellowship President Chuck Colson, this woman had no inclination to forgive Ron Flowers. On the contrary, she harbored only hatred for this convicted killer, understandably. The fifteen years he had served so far in a Texas prison were for the murder of Mrs. Washington's daughter. But one day something changed. Here's how Colson recounted it.

> I witnessed an example of this [spiritual] power recently when I visited . . . a wing of a Texas prison, run by Prison Fellowship. Prayers have replaced early-morning push-ups, while group Bible studies have pre-empted evening MTV. . . .
>
> I dropped in on a class on drug and alcohol prevention to hear one of the inmates say, "I've been in three therapy programs, and they don't work, because I'm back in prison." Then he added, "We're not interested in therapy. We're interested in transformation." The room resounded with Amens. . . .
>
> But the most breathtaking moment in my visit came during a graduation ceremony for inmates who had completed the entire 18-month program. As an inmate approached me for his certificate, out of the corner of my eye I saw a tall, stately woman rise from her seat among the visitors. Her name was Mrs. Washington, and she swept to the front, wrapped her arms around the inmate, and declared to everyone, "This young man is my adopted son." . . .
>
> Arriving at this moment had not been easy for either of them. Ron Flowers had maintained his innocence during 15 years in prison. Then he joined the Sycamore Tree project (a Prison Fellowship program that helps offenders confess their wrongs and make restitution to their victims), and for the first time he admitted his crime and prayed that his victim's family would forgive him.
>
> On her side, every year of Ron's sentence Mrs. Washington had written angry letters to the parole board, urging them to deny him parole. But the same week that Ron confessed, strangely, Mrs. Washington had felt an overwhelming conviction that she was to forgive the man who had murdered her daughter. The next day, she wrote the board that she no longer opposed Ron's parole. She then tracked Ron down to express her forgiveness.[4]

Mrs. Washington's forgiveness came before she knew or had any reason to expect that her daughter's killer had confessed or intended to seek her forgiveness. Just like Jesus. Hers is the kind of extreme case that gives us hope in finding the capacity to forgive even when the prospect of doing so seems light-years beyond our ability to do so.

Can the offer of forgiveness be abused? You bet it can. However, the call to forgive is an essential for every healthy marriage. The marriage vows I ask couples to repeat as they exchange rings include the statement "I will forgive you when you fail." Note that I don't say "*if* you fail," but "*when* you fail." No marriage is free of failure. Therefore, every partner in marriage must learn to forgive, even if it is abused.

The one who takes advantage of a forgiving spouse will answer to God someday for abusing the gift of grace. But the one who withholds grace, fearful it might be abused, will stand accountable to the same God of grace. So give it generously, just as it is delivered daily to you from above.

NOTES

1. Lewis Smedes, *Forgive and Forget* (New York: Pocket, Simon & Schuster, 1984), 45.

2. Ibid., 47.

3. Ibid., 53.

4. Adapted from *Jubilee* magazine, winter 1999, © 1999, reprinted with permission of Prison Fellowship Ministries, P.O. Box 17500, Washington, D.C. 10041-0500.

CHAPTER EIGHT

MARRIAGE: ROUTINE MAINTENANCE REQUIRED

Marriages in America are in trouble today. It's time we face that fact. Just look at these statistics:

- More than 16 million Americans are divorced today.
- Forty percent of Christian marriages will be touched in some way by infidelity by the time the couple reaches the age of forty.
- Sixteen to 20 percent of pastors say they have been sexually inappropriate with a member of the opposite sex.
- The fastest-rising percentage of extramarital affairs today is among young women. Rising at an alarming rate are those who have been married five years or less.
- Fifty-eight percent of all women and 68 percent of all men have engaged in some form of sexual indiscretion during their lives and at times have stepped over the line in an inappropriate way with someone to whom they're not married.

Behind each of these statistics are countless stories of marriages gone to seed. And the most common reaction I hear from men and women who wake up and find themselves included in these percentages is "I never thought that would happen to me," or "I never dreamed I would do that." This is especially true among Christians. Worse yet, many of these people have no idea what went wrong. "It's as if I woke up," one man told me, "and suddenly realized that the love was gone and I couldn't recover."

Joe, or so we'll call him, was somewhere between desperation and despair when I first heard him utter those words in my office. His wife had just discovered that another woman had invaded the domain of their marriage. His affair was not a one-night fall but a long-term slide from which he felt helpless to recover. He never meant to be unfaithful. The thought of it disgusted him. Other guys do "that," but not him. His wife was attractive, wonderful to him, and a great mom to their kids. He had the new home in the preferred new subdivision. He had climbed his corporate ladder faster than anyone in the company. His future was bright, almost blinding.

This affair with a coworker, though, had put it all on the line. He could lose his wife, his home, his reputation, even his job. Yet he felt trapped. Innocent expressions of appreciation, admiration, and respect had blossomed into affection outside the boundaries of his marriage vows. Those affections stirred passions he had only faintly remembered from earlier years with his wife. Those passions and the affair that grew from them had now taken control of his life. They had lied to him. The brief moments of pleasure were delivered only at the price of an endless season of pain. And most of all, he saw no easy way out. His heart, life, and marriage were divided and at risk of being destroyed.

A PERTINENT PARABLE IN A PROVERB

Stowed away in the wisdom of Solomon is a piece of gear that should be standard issue for every man and woman—every Martian and Venusian—who launches on a marriage mission. It's actually a parable, out of which we can extract a proverb that will flow into several principles that we can apply to the marriage relationship. It is especially relevant if we wish to avoid the pain and marital destruction I have just described. Listen to some old wisdom that still speaks life today.

I passed by the field of the sluggard
And by the vineyard of the man lacking sense,
And behold, it was completely overgrown with thistles;
Its surface was covered with nettles,
And its stone wall was broken down.
When I saw, I reflected upon it;
I looked, and received instruction.
                              —Proverbs 24:30–32

And as this man on a journey reflected and observed, God gave him instruction that goes way beyond mere gardening.

"A little sleep, a little slumber,
A little folding of the hands to rest,"
Then your poverty will come as a robber
And your want like an armed man.
                              —Proverbs 24:33–34

If you look closely at the parable recounted in this proverb, you'll find a *cause,* a *result,* and a *warning* that provide powerfully practical counsel for couples who are interested in building and maintaining strong marriages.

The cause. We've all seen a home that's run-down and in total disrepair. We've all seen fields or gardens that have been entirely overrun by weeds. What causes something to deteriorate to such a condition? "A little sleep, a little slumber, a little folding of the hands to rest" answers this question. It's a person who is slow to get out of bed, slow to work on something that needs attention, too lazy to do routine maintenance. And notice the key word, which is repeated not once but three times. "A *little* sleep, a *little* slumber, a *little* folding of the hands to rest," and *total* destruction soon follows. It's the *little* bit of neglect that brings a *whole lot* of ruin. We get a clear correlation to this concept in Proverbs 26:14. Concerning this man, the sluggard, it says:

As the door turns on its hinges,
So does the sluggard on his bed.

Isn't that a great analogy? In other words, it's saying this isn't a guy who won't work at all, but he likes to put his work off. He tends to neglect things. He just doesn't jump on them when he should. He has a bad habit of rolling over, hitting the snooze button time after time after time. He's not a bad guy, just a *little* lazy. He always figures he can wait a *little* longer before he kicks into gear and tackles his day. If he had a favorite T-shirt, it would have one word printed on it: LATER.

Proverbs 24:30 says, "I passed by . . . the vineyard of the man lacking sense." Not only was this guy lazy, but he lacked wisdom. In fact, if you look closely at the Hebrew term that's translated here as "lacking sense," you find that it could be rendered "lacking heart." He has little motivation. We're talking about a guy who's lacking wisdom and initiative. So he's not grossly immoral. He's not necessarily a wicked man or a rebel. In fact, he's a nice guy. The neighbor next door. The all-American, average "gardener" who is just a *little* short on initiative, wisdom, and motivation. We've all known him or her. In fact, at times we've all *been* him or her.

The result. It doesn't take a doctorate in horticulture to figure out the fate of this guy's vineyard. It fell into complete ruin. "It was completely overgrown," according to the text, wiped out by thorns, thistles, and nettles to the point that there was no hope of ever recovering it. And when a vineyard is that far gone, when the weeds have taken control, you only have one option: Torch it. Light a match, burn it up, and start all over. Or worse yet, just walk away and abandon it.

Unfortunately, the picture gets worse. In that part of Israel, stone walls were typically built around vineyards to both keep out predators and define the boundaries of one person's vineyard as opposed to another's. In this parable, that stone wall was also broken down. Stone by stone it had crumbled because nobody was maintaining it. Again, it didn't happen overnight in an earthquake. It happened slowly, one stone at a time. The owner had to notice, but he thought, *What's one stone going to matter? I'll get to it later.* (There's that T-shirt again.) So the picture we have here is one of complete and utter ruin brought about by putting things off.

The warning. We can easily extract a warning from this story, a principle worth remembering. It's that *procrastination leads to devastation.* Just waiting, failing to act when we should, while we can, when something really needs our attention, can have calamitous results. A little neglect over a long period of time can lead to a lot of ruin. Proverbs 24:34 gives us a memorable word picture to help us understand the degree of devastation we're talking about here. "Then your poverty will come as a robber and your want like an armed man." In other words, you can't stop this ruination.

It's like going to bed thinking everything is OK, but when you wake up somebody has cleaned you out, and there's nothing you can do about it. We're talking swift, unexpected, irreversible destruction here. It feels like a robber swooped in and took all we had, but in reality, the wall came down slowly, stone by stone. The weeds came up, took over, and choked out the vineyard, one plant at a time. "A little sleep, a little slumber, a little folding of the hands to rest." Not full retirement. Just a little rest.

When I contemplate the message of this story, I think of people whose relationships have fallen apart, whose marriages have fallen into disrepair. So often the answer to the question, "What really caused that marriage to fall apart?" isn't so much the final, explosive event that announced the couple's troubles to all the world. It's the fact that over the years, "a little sleep, a little slumber, a little folding of the hands to rest" took place. What's true of a vineyard is true of a marriage. A little neglect leads to a lot of ruin.

A number of years ago, my wife Becky and I bought a home in Ohio. We were excited about our "new" place, an 1890s farmhouse, for a lot of reasons. One was that nestled beside it was the richest, most beautiful garden plot in the whole county. We knew this because we had driven past that particular house many times. Every spring nearly half of the two acres of land around the house was tilled and planted. The soil was meticulously prepared for planting. And this garden wasn't just big; it was well tended. As a result, every summer its soft, rich black earth yielded the biggest ears of corn and the richest-looking produce you've ever seen. It was a beautiful garden.

So when we bought that house we were doubly thrilled because we got the garden in the deal. And the next year we plowed up the ground and planted enough food to feed half the people in the county. Once we had everything in the ground and growing, though, our summer schedule kicked into high gear. First we had to run our annual youth camp for three weeks. Then came two weeks of family vacation. By the time we returned home, something terribly unexpected had happened to our garden. The vegetables were all gone! Oh, they were there somewhere, but totally obscured by a crop of weeds that was absolutely demonic in its dimension. I mean, these things were huge. The corn may have been shoulder high, but the weeds were way over our heads. Our supersoil had grown the very best, greenest, healthiest weed patch in the state, maybe in the country!

We tried to eradicate the intruders, but our efforts were futile. Our lovely garden was an eyesore, overgrown and beyond recovering. Just like the sluggard in Proverbs, we just had to give up and let it go. And at the end of the year we set a torch to one corner of the garden and watched the flames consume the whole thing. Now that I think about it, those weeds were so out of control that when we set them on fire the flames actually licked the telephone lines that ran overhead.

That big old garden comes to mind whenever I read this little proverb. "A little sleep, a little slumber." That's all it takes. Just ignore the weeds and guess what? They multiply. They set their roots deep down and before long you're facing total ruin.

What's the point of this proverb? Simply this: *A little neglect of what could be easily fixed can lead, seemingly without warning, to problems that at least appear to be beyond repair.* This warning is not only true, but timeless. It's equally applicable to vineyards, to gardens, and to marriages. The good news is that with some regular, routine maintenance, you can keep the weeds away, leaving plenty of room for your marriage garden's plants to grow strong and produce good fruit.

TIPS FOR ROUTINE MAINTENANCE

What can you do to keep from becoming one of the statistics mentioned at the beginning of this chapter? Or, if your story is already reflected in those statistics, what can you learn today from God to help you in a new relationship? I think we can glean at least four lessons from this proverb.

Keep close watch on the garden. This may seem like "Horticulture 101," but don't discount its importance. Good maintenance that results in great fruitfulness begins with attentiveness. One year after the big burn off next to our farmhouse, we had a beautiful garden. The secret? We leased our plot of super earth to a friend who lived in town and had almost no room to exercise his passion for growing vegetables. It was a great arrangement. He got free use of our premier garden spot and we got free pickin's from the fruit of his labor. When harvesttime came for various delectable delights, he'd even leave bags of goodies on our doorstep!

Why did he reap the harvest when we had simply enjoyed a bonfire one short year earlier? Attentiveness was the key. He visited the garden often, not just once a day but twice. At sunrise he'd walk in there plucking some produce and pulling a few weeds that dared to invade his turf. He wasn't there long, but he knew every plant by name. At times I thought I saw him talking to them. He'd often return with his family in the evening for a second look around. He stayed in the know and in touch with his prized plot of ground.

So what's the connection to marriage? Marriage is like a garden. It needs to be watched and maintained as a prized possession. But the first step toward effective maintenance is attentive monitoring. Marriages, like gardens, do not go to seed or become overrun overnight. So just as the gardener is on the lookout for early signs of trouble, so the husband and wife must stay attentive to evidence of a wilting love relationship. Here are a few tips for pulling this off.

Make sure you keep the communication lines open. Talk about needs and expectations often. Too frequently we assume one of two things, often with the same destructive result. One is that we think our spouse will intuitively know our needs, which seldom happens. The other mistake is to assume that when we do express what we want or need, we're using words or actions that actually convey our message clearly. In either case, the adage about the dangers of assuming comes into play.

Let's use a simple example to illustrate. Suppose that when you got married, only one of you worked outside the home, but now you're both holding down full-time jobs. As the newcomer to the workforce and the one who's also been accustomed to taking care of many of the responsibilities at home, you've tried to keep doing those household chores alone—after your long day at the office. Things like making dinner, doing the dishes, and cleaning up the kitchen. It's become quickly apparent, to *you* at least, that you now need this to be a shared responsibility. But your spouse seems to be content to follow his or her old routine of crashing after work in front of the tube or behind the newspaper or both (in which case you wonder if your mate has X-ray vision but never ask).

If your home is like ours, the typical way for a woman to bring up this issue would probably be different from how a man would do it. Most guys would likely take the direct route, something like, "Honey, taking care of most things around the house was a whole lot easier when I wasn't working. Now, though, it's just too much. How about if we talk about splitting up what needs to be done? Maybe we switch off doing dinner and cleaning up after. What do you think?"

A woman, on the other hand, might come at it more indirectly. Maybe she hides the remote, but he buys a backup. She sighs deeply while doing the dishes and mentions how hard her day was, to which he replies thoughtfully through the newspaper, "Uh-huh." When he fails to jump in and help, she is convinced that he doesn't love her or really care about her needs. Women are genetically engineered to believe the number one maxim of marriage: "If you cared, you'd notice."

So she begins to feel bitter and finally says, "Have you noticed that I still do everything I used to do before taking my job, and I go to work from 8 A.M. to 5 P.M. every day?" To which he declares through the newspaper, "Yes, you are marvelous, sweetheart."

At that moment a major weed sprouts in the garden! As she blows and storms out of the room, he hunkers down on the couch for the night and wonders, *What's bothering her?* He recovers his courage and ventures into the bedroom, which, strangely enough, feels like the inside of a freezer, and says something profound like, "Is something wrong, honey?" to which she replies, "Well, since we're both gone all day now, it would be nice if you offered to pitch in and help with things after we get home."

At which point the guy wouldn't be atypical if he said something insensitively obvious like, "I'm sorry; I didn't even think of that. Why didn't you ask me?" And of course she wouldn't be unusual if she assumed he was intentionally overlooking the obvious and replied, "Well, I don't feel like I should have to ask you." (You can complete this dialogue if you like.)

With so many variables to complicate a simple situation like this, you can see how important it is that couples keep talking—openly, honestly, and clearly. Never assume the other person gets it or knows what your needs are. Fact is, when men and women (sorry, but especially us guys) fell in the first garden (Eden), man (and some would say women as well) fell right on the antennae that are necessary for picking up the coded signals of the opposite sex. It's one more way we are different by design. So keep checking the condition of the garden.

That's the admonishment in Ephesians 4:15, where we're challenged to be "speaking the truth in love," and verse 25, where we're urged to "speak truth each one of you with his neighbor." As we mentioned earlier, there's no neighbor closer than the person you married. If the three keys to real estate are location, location, location, you could say that the three keys to marriage are communication, communication, communication!

Also keep in mind that not only will your needs differ, but the way men and women process things is dramatically different as well. If something Becky does or says hurts me, I'm likely to let her know—now. Becky, on the other hand, may not let on right away and wait for an "ideal" moment to tell me what's up. In either case, if we don't learn to speak clearly when we're talking about our feelings and our needs, then we'll probably get in trouble.

Disappointment is another emotion that men and women tend to handle differently. If a high school football team loses a big game, it's not uncommon for the cheerleaders, who are as emotionally involved in the game as the players on the field, to cry. The guys, on the other hand, might be more inclined to suck it up, or get angry or simply write it off as a best effort that wasn't good enough on this particular day. These differing responses to the same phenomenon can easily be misread by guys and girls. If a cheerleader is dating one of the players, that doubles the trouble. He's angry when they get together after the game; she might think she did something to set him off. He could get the same impression from her tears, and both would be completely wrong.

The example may be simplistic, but the point applies in the most complicated of miscommunications in a marriage. *Never assume.* Make sure you let your spouse know exactly what's going on, and keep in mind that your needs in a similar situation may be entirely different.

The best example I can think of to drive this point home is the way men and women typically process problems. If a guy comes home from work, for instance, complaining about something he's dealing with at the office, he's looking for one thing from his wife. Respect. He knows she can't fix the problem. He just needs to hear her say that she knows *he* can fix the problem. If her response is something like, "Bud, don't worry about it. You can handle that. Don't give it another thought. You can do it," then he's OK. He's excited to get back the next day and prove her right. And he appreciates her.

Now, if that woman comes home the next day and unloads on him a big problem she's facing, and he responds to her like she responded to him, look out. She does not want to hear, "Oh, honey, don't worry about it. That thing will probably take care of itself, and if it doesn't, you can handle it." He hasn't helped the situation at all by responding this way. In fact, he's probably in trouble with his wife if he does. She doesn't want his respect at that moment. She wants to know that he cares for her. And believe it or not, if he just listens, she gets that important message. By listening he affirms her, he validates her feelings and he lets her know he loves her.

When it comes to loving your spouse, keep in mind that preventive maintenance begins with keeping a watchful eye on the garden. If both husband and wife are watching for the weeds and working the garden together, then they'll both share in some great feasts.

FERTILIZE WHAT YOU WANT TO GROW

Every vinedresser knows what it takes to make his vines grow strong and produce plump, juicy grapes. Preventive maintenance is certainly essential for sustaining a healthy environment. In a marriage as in the vineyard, though, it's also vital to fertilize what we want to grow. The goal is a healthy, fruitful relationship. And I've found several old standbys that are still the best for boosting the yield in your marriage.

One is liberal applications of *appreciation*. Say "Thank you" often, not just for the big things, but for little ones as well. Let the one you love know that you notice his or her expressions of love and that you're grateful for them. To do so conveys not only appreciation but also respect. With the pace of life today, it's too easy to roll through the day, each doing his own thing and never pausing to notice, much less acknowledge, his mate's efforts at making their marriage work.

Another proven enhancer of marital health and growth is to water regularly with *praise*. Phrases like "I love it, honey, when you . . ." and "I admire you so much for . . ." and "I'm so proud of you and the way you . . ." both esteem and encourage your partner when expressed genuinely and at the right times. Philippians 4:8 is a direct commandment for every person, including husbands and wives, to do this: "If there is . . . anything worthy of praise, dwell on these things." And if I could be so bold as to add, "Let your mind dwell on these things and let them spill out of your mouth." Be liberal in your praise for one another and watch your marriage grow.

Couples often ask me how they should respond if their spouse is, let's say, "deficient" in certain areas. "How do I change my husband?" or "What can I do to help my wife change?" are common questions. I always offer a two-part response. First, don't nag and expect results. That's like kicking at the dirt in those areas of a garden that aren't producing well. The result in the garden is even more irritation, with less productive plants. In a marriage you get the same outcome—more frustration and less to show for it. The alternative is to look for the strengths in your spouse and nurture them. Praise your wife for who she is and what she does well. Let your husband know that you notice those aspects of his character and behavior that contribute to your relationship. My guess is you'll start to see growth in other areas as well.

Remember that *acts of kindness* will also enrich the soil, causing the romance and the relationship to bloom. And by the way, this secret soil conditioner is most effective when applied before the garden demands it. In other words, surprise your spouse by helping, assisting, taking on that project he or she has wanted done *before* she starts dropping hints or he begins making demands. Men, what one single act would shock your wife—in a good sense? Just do it and watch the response. Ladies, what could you do, what one loving surprise could you present to him, that would blow your husband away? Go ahead and see if he doesn't love you for it.

Simple gifts also qualify as relationship sweeteners. They don't have to cost a lot, just say a lot. When I was a young pastor, there was seldom room for flowers in our budget. A dozen roses didn't come cheap, even back then. But then I discovered "the bucket," the white plastic pail at the supermarket where the florist placed flowers that were on their last legs, about to be thrown out. A whole bunch for a couple of bucks! Becky loved them and never asked where they came from (although I'm sure she knew). More importantly, she knew that I cared.

Remember our proverb: "A little sleep, a little slumber, a little folding of the hands to rest" (Proverbs 24:33). Take this approach and you're asking for trouble. Practice preventive maintenance, though, and watch your relationship grow. Communicate your needs and expectations. Fertilize with liberal, regular doses of appreciation, praise, and kindness. And notice that I said *regular* doses. Apply a little fertilizer each day. Don't wait until the end of the month or the end of a season to dump a whole truckload of fertilizer and expect good results. Anyone who's visited a true working farm knows that too much "fresh" fertilizer can actually cause a stink! Too much of any good thing can have the opposite effect intended.

WATCH OUT FOR WEEDS

Every garden, just like that big one Becky and I planted back in Ohio, grows weeds as well as vegetables. Every marriage does too. And the biblical warning is clear. Pull them out quickly before they take root and do some real damage. "Do not let the sun go down on your anger" (Ephesians 4:26). Don't let that weed stay in your garden overnight. If you don't deal with it, two things are sure to happen. It'll take root, and it'll multiply.

One particularly pesky weed, bitterness, starts like most others—as a seed. You know it's landed in the soil around your heart when you begin to notice thoughts like *I'm just feeling kind of bugged by her today,* or, *It kind of irritates me that he. . . .* If something is bothering you, the worst thing you can do is ignore it. Then that seed of bitterness begins to send down roots. And when left to grow unchecked, those roots can become nearly impossible to pull out.

We see the most extreme cases of this phenomenon in places like Kosovo and Ireland and the Middle East, places where roots of bitterness have grown so long and gone so deep that people who are hating and fighting may not even know the origin of their animosity. I know a couple whose life together allowed patches of bitterness to take root over the years to the point that the wife so resented her husband's minor offenses that she took to sleeping on the sofa every night but never told him why. If something your spouse is or isn't doing is bugging you or hurting you, don't ignore it. Get it out in the open and get rid of it.

Another wicked weed is *unfaithfulness.* This drops into our minds as little seeds of lustful thoughts toward people outside our marriage, thoughts that we naively dismiss as harmless. It is those same seeds, though, that germinate into discontent and blossom into deadly affairs. "Watch over your heart with all diligence," Proverbs 4:23 advises, "for from it flow the springs of life." We do well to take these words seriously and pay attention to the way weeds like unfaithfulness invade our marriages. As I reflect on the weeds in our gardens and our marriages, at least five similarities come to mind. These should encourage us to never ignore those weeds when they begin to sprout.

Weeds that hurt your marriage always start below the surface. Most marriages fail because early on something went wrong in a spouse's heart and he or she didn't deal with it. You have to maintain a healthy heart, and that involves guarding against bad seeds even getting into it. Patrol your thought life, because that's where the seeds come in. Decide early on what you will and won't listen to or read or watch. Make yourselves accountable to one another in this area of life, and to at least one other husband or wife. To do so is as wise as installing an antivirus program on your computer to keep your files from being corrupted. For the gardener it's like the product Halts® or a similar lawn treatment. The chemical actually prevents seeds from even germinating. When I guard my thought life, sin never gets a chance to sprout.

Weeds and sin that destroy marriages appeal to the senses. At least in the early stages, the things capable of causing the most damage to your union will look and even smell nice. I don't know about your part of the country, but where I come from, the most common weed in my backyard was the dandelion. Where we live in California, it's oxalis, a cloverlike weed with small blossoms. Both have lovely flowers, but they spread like mad and take over a lawn. They look good at first, but then they spread and wreck everything.

When it comes to the weeds that are destructive to marriage, there's also the *pleasure* factor. A rough paraphrase of Hebrews

11:24–26 would be "Moses chose to live righteously rather than to enjoy the passing pleasures of sin." One of the reasons sin is so tempting is that it frequently feels so good. It smells wonderful and looks so attractive. You see, playing around outside your marriage, simply enjoying a mental or emotional affair with someone, may look appealing on the surface. It brings a little joy, a little excitement. It appeals to your senses. And like those common weeds in your yard, they often get started when the grass is a little thin, weak, or undernourished. Unfortunately, those same senses are incapable of telling you that this temporary pleasure will eventually give way to long-term pain. Don't take the bait.

Weeds left to grow develop deep roots. And weeds with deep roots are neither easily removed nor readily disposed of. Once you finally get them out you'll face the consequences of having let them get established in the first place. For men, it may be lustful thoughts that progress to pornography or adultery. For women, the progression might be from anger or bitterness to aloofness and an affair. Maybe it's money troubles—impulsiveness on the part of husband or wife that escalates into overspending or gambling. Whatever the outcome, when weeds are allowed to do their dirty work, you'll have more pain and heartache than you bargained for on the front end when it comes time to clean up after the fact.

Weeds spread quickly beyond the borders. The word used at the nursery is *invasive*. Weeds, by their very nature, aren't content to stay in their place. They want more of the turf. More control. They suck up more and more of the moisture and nutrients needed for healthy plants. Sin, especially relational sin, is truly invasive as well. One thing I've noticed is how anger affects me. If I'm feeling angry at Becky for something and I haven't talked with her about it, then trouble starts showing up in the weirdest places. I begin reading her actions through this anger filter, and suddenly things that normally wouldn't bother me start ticking me off. Pretty soon everything Becky says can be distorted to look like it's intended to hurt me. Is that true in your life? Proverbs warns us that "the beginning of strife is like letting out water, so abandon the quarrel before it breaks out" (17:14). Whatever the weed, whatever the sin you allow into one area of your marriage—lust, bitterness, discontent —it will eventually spread and threaten your entire relationship.

Weeds choke out a marriage. The obvious upshot of the previous point is that weeds left unchecked won't stop until they've ruined the entire garden. Unresolved bitterness will rob you of the good fruit of joy in your marriage. The joy won't be able to get the light it needs to flourish, or the moisture or nutrients, because your bitterness is in the way. Emotional energy that you should be investing in your love relationship will be siphoned away to sustain the weeds' destructive influence.

This is why I counsel both men and women to never use a member of the opposite sex, other than your mate, as a means of meeting your emotional needs. Mr. Martian, never pour out your problems to a Venusian at the office. Mrs. Venusian, do not make that Martian friend the confidant who empathizes with your marital woes. Do that and before long you won't have the emotional energy to reclaim the type of intimacy God wants you to have with your spouse. Then you'll look back and wonder why your love died, and you won't even realize that you fed the weed instead of fertilizing the plant God gave you. The love that you thought died had actually been starved to death.

KEEP YOUR WALLS IN GOOD REPAIR

"And its stone wall was broken down" (Proverbs 24:31). As I think of this image in Proverbs, of the wall around the vineyard having crumbled from neglect, I cringe. Walls were built around vineyards for a reason: to keep out predators and anything else that might do damage to the highly valued vines growing within the safety of their protection. The correlation to marriage is clear.

Strong walls help focus your affections. Looking first from inside the walls, consider this. Strong, clear borders in your marriage, like walls around a vineyard, help you focus your affections. Distractions are kept at a safe distance, which allows you to concentrate on your relationship with the person inside the walls. When I'm reminded often that Becky is the intended focus of my affections, I recognize other women as being outside the walls. To jump over the wall, to blow through the boundaries that we've set up to protect our marriage, is inappropriate.

Make sure you keep clear boundaries around your marriage. "Drink water from your own cistern and fresh water from your own well," Proverbs says (5:15), and "Let your fountain be blessed, and rejoice in the wife of your youth" (5:18).

Strong walls protect you from temptation. Strong boundaries also protect you from outside predators that would wreck your relationship. Our culture, like every other, is full of predatory people. There are men and women who are emotionally starved, and if you're a compassionate, loving person, in the workplace, for example, they will be attracted to you because they'll sense that you're someone who cares about people. On one level, that's great! If you're a Christian, it may even be an opportunity to tell someone about Jesus' love for them. But don't let your evangelistic zeal create a crack in the wall that allows a relationship to become such that it would wreck your life and ruin your marriage. Don't take on an assignment in someone else's vineyard that you have no business doing. Early on, in an "evangelistic relationship" with someone of the opposite sex, I seek to involve another friend of the same sex or even my wife.

How do you maintain the integrity of the walls around your marriage? Let's say you're around a member of the opposite sex who is obviously attractive, who has a sweet personality, and who is, frankly, fun to be around. Maybe you even pick up some signals that that person is attracted to you. When something like this is going on, do what we've told our adolescent kids to do. Make your important decisions ahead of time, before you're in a situation where it's more difficult to do so. In this case, decide ahead of time that you'll never be alone with that person.

Some would respond by saying, "Hey, get real. I work with this person. We have to be together at times." OK, make sure there's a picture of your husband or wife on your desk or in the room. Speak about your spouse. Brag about her or him. To do so is to shore up the wall around your relationship. When I talk about Becky to another woman, that's exactly what I'm doing. Conversely, if I criticize my wife to another woman, I might as well hang a sign on my chest that says, "I'm available!" Never criticize your spouse to anyone, especially a member of the opposite sex. Dealing with those issues is reserved for the safety and privacy of your own walls.

I recently heard an astonishing story about a wall that reminded me of the importance of maintaining good ones. A friend's next-door neighbors were selling their home and, as is customary in California, the buyer hired an inspector to give the place a thorough going-over. There was no reason to suspect any problems; several walk-throughs with the realtor had left the buyers with the same impression the sellers had—that the home was solid. In a state where earthquakes are common, that was reassuring.

The inspector was confirming the home's structural strength when he came to one particular interior wall. A slight telltale sign prompted him to do a little probing, and what he found beneath the drywall shocked everyone. Dry rot had literally destroyed the two-by-four framing of the wall. When they peeled the wallboard off, they found shriveled black strands where solid wood had once been. The drywall was essentially supporting itself. Repairs to the home were both extensive and costly.

Building walls around your marriage is only the beginning of preserving a healthy union. Make sure you do regular maintenance too. And if there's even a hint of structural damage, probe quickly and as deeply as necessary to uncover the problem and correct it.

Remember, "a little sleep, a little slumber, a little folding of the hands to rest" . . . and your marriage can face the total ruin of divorce. Don't make the mistake of avoiding routine maintenance in your marriage. Be sure to

- Keep close watch on your garden.
- Fertilize what you want to grow.
- Watch out for weeds.
- Keep your walls in good repair.

Let me close with a final practical tip. Along with your daily and weekly routine maintenance, devote one week or weekend per year to an annual marriage "tune-up." Just as it's a good investment to take your car in for that once-over with the mechanic . . . just as it's a good practice to see your physician for an annual checkup . . . it's also a great idea to get away as a couple. No kids, no pets, no pressure. Just the two of you getting away for some fun and to evaluate the state of your garden. This is one investment that can reap a bumper crop in your marriage, if you'll let it.

CHAPTER NINE

WHAT DO YOU MEAN WHEN YOU SAY "I DO"?

We've all been there. It's one of the few occasions in our "don't sweat it if you're late" culture when you try to arrive early.

You know the drill. You sign in with a feathery pen and are escorted to your seat by some ordinary guys who look extraordinarily sharp in their rented tuxedos. Of course, the place smells like a floral shop. Just as the last candle is being lit, a voice-for-hire soloist or close-though-marginally-musically-talented friend belts out a generic love song or whatever tune happens to be hottest on the marital music charts. As the solo ends, the organist begins playing one of those familiar melodies chosen for both its beauty and its centuries-old track record for setting exactly the right pace for bridal attendants to march gracefully down the aisle. You scramble to identify who's who, matching faces with the list of names in the printed program.

The last one steps to her assigned spot as a chuckle and a few "Oohs" and "Ahhs" ripple through the room. A preschool sister or niece scatters rose petals down the aisle while her self-conscious ring-bearing escort shuffles stiffly beside her. As they reach the front, the music increases in volume, so you know what's coming. The mother of the bride stands and all rise as if doing the wave at the big game. They turn in unison to see the bride, veiled and as lovely as she has ever looked, on the arm of her proud but terrified father. He knows that, of all his assignments as a dad, he'd better get this one right.

The exchange takes place and Dad takes a seat beside his wife (who he notices also looks especially radiant today). At this point, you probably tune out the next few minutes as the officiant goes through the wedding routine. If you're a guy, you're wondering what's on the menu at the reception. If you're a woman, you tune out for a different reason. You're comparing the colors of the bridesmaids' dresses with their bouquets and the guys' bow ties and cummerbunds. You're thinking, "This ceremony is like all the other weddings I've ever attended" (including your own) when these words snap you back to the here and now . . .

"Do you, John, take Mary to be your lawfully wedded wife, to have and to hold from this day forward, for better or for worse, in sickness and in health, for richer and for poorer, to love and to cherish, as long as you both shall live?" Whether he hesitates or speaks before the pastor finishes or whispers to his bride or shouts for the whole audience to hear, you know what's coming: "I do." Then it's the bride's turn. "Do you, Mary, take John this day, in the presence of God, to be your lawfully wedded husband . . . as long as you both shall live?" Her "I do" usually comes with less hesitation, and after a few more familiar phrases, a quick kiss, and a joyful exit, the ceremony is over. You head for the door, eager to get in on the food and fun at the reception, hoping the pictures won't take too long.

This scenario is replayed regularly in various forms and locations across America. My fear is that we know it so well, maybe even have it memorized, but we don't understand either its significance or its substance. Americans often view the marriage vows as mere legal or religious formalities that have to be dispensed with before the party can begin. Or maybe they just consider them to be part of our cultural tradition, like singing the national anthem before a ball game or saying the pledge of allegiance at the start of a school day.

But what should it mean—what *does* it mean to say such things to a person in the presence of God? What does God do during the wedding? Is He, like us, merely a spectator? Do we really believe He is there and listening and even recording our promises in His omniscient book of vows?

The Book of Common Prayer, originally published by the Church of England and ratified in 1789 by the Protestant Episcopal Church in the United States of America, contains not only prayers, but also these vows in a section entitled "The Marriage."

> "In the name of God, I, John, take you, Mary, to be my wife, to have and to hold from this day forward, for better for worse, for richer for poorer, in sickness and in health, to love and to cherish, until we are parted by death. This is my solemn vow."

These words are still the point of reference for virtually every Christian couple as they craft the vows they will recite at the altar. If these are vows made to God, in His presence, with the witness of family and friends, don't you think it's important that we understand not only what we pledge but why we pledge it?

One of the best-read people I know is my friend and former ministry associate Paul Sailhamer. Frankly, I've always found it a bit intimidating that in a day when many people feel like they're doing well if they read a few books a year, it is not uncommon for Paul to have five or six books going at any one time. This man is definitely a disciplined reader, and one by-product of his discipline is a conviction that I share as a student and teacher of the Bible. "Words have meanings," Paul is quick to remind, especially when people are inclined to be lazy about what they're writing or saying.

I know, this sounds so obvious as to hardly be worth saying. But we violate it all the time by choosing words carelessly, using words when we're not sure of their meanings, failing to notice when long-accepted meanings of words change and, worst of all, refusing to take the meanings of words seriously (which typically results in the equally disturbing practice of redefining words to fit our preferences). A few examples (courtesy of Paul Sailhamer):

lucky • Christian people often use it, then feel uncomfortable with its implications and substitute "fortunate," which Sailhamer points out is a word that derives from the Latin word for . . . you guessed it, lucky.

experience • too often misused as a noun which takes the focus off the verb that should predominate, as in "Let's have a worship experience" (versus "Let's worship").

wedding • another noun that, when coupled with "experience," creates a compound which fuels our tendency to forget that it's the verb "to wed" which should be our focus, a verb which means, by the way, to trade promises.

See what I mean? Not only do words have meanings, but certain words, spoken at certain times, carry with them a depth and breadth of meaning that cannot be ignored. Such is the case with wedding vows. Think about it. We attend weddings all the time, and we've all heard our share of vows being exchanged. As a result, we're in danger of becoming so familiar with the words spoken before a couple says "I do" that we either tune out, don't think about them, or don't know what they mean. When it comes to one word that is inherent in wedding vows, traditional or otherwise, this is particularly perilous. It is a word we not only cannot ignore but must explore. That word is *covenant*.

MARRIAGE: CONTRACT OR COVENANT?

It used to be that contracts were settled with a handshake, and, once agreed upon, were binding. No more. Just take a look at the sports pages. How often have you heard that a guy with X number of years left on his contract got traded or made it abundantly clear that he wanted to play for a different team? As prevalent as the problem is in professional athletics, it's not fair to lay all the blame there. The problem predates the twentieth century. Native Americans discovered the unreliability of written contracts when they signed treaties with the United States government. Every century evidences this very human tendency to say one thing and then do another when it becomes convenient, expedient, or simply easier than keeping your word.

In fact, the root of the problem isn't found in any culture or country, any generation or gender, but in the human heart itself. Like many of his generation, my high school football coach used to say: "When the going gets tough, the tough get going." But unfortunately, when it comes to modern-day marriages, the tough literally do often "get going" when the going gets tough. They hit the road. Instead of jumping in, they are bailing out in record numbers. Last time I checked, the national divorce rate was pushing 60 percent.

It used to be that things like personal religious belief, the general social stigma of divorce, the societal conviction that it was honorable to simply hang in there, and the pure economics of the family combined to work against divorce. No more. In our twenty-first-century world, each of these deterrents has evaporated. People who hold a faith that leads to real conviction are harder to find. The stigma of divorce has diminished dramatically. And most families in America now reflect dual careers with dual incomes, which means one spouse can bail on the other and still be financially independent. I meet more and more couples these days who even keep separate assets and bank accounts.

Granted, some of these cultural shifts do have an upside. It's good, for example, that those who have suffered through a failed marriage, or perhaps have experienced abuse or infidelity, are not shunned by the church. They need the love and acceptance of God's people and the healing power of His grace. It is good, too, that women today are more respected and rewarded for their skills in the workplace. The wife in Proverbs 31 certainly was! But today's culture not only grants permission for divorce (as Scripture does in limited cases in Matthew 19 and 1 Corinthians 7), but it actually encourages couples to call it quits.

I'll never forget the couple who showed up in my office weekly trying to patch up their seven-year-old marriage which, while in trouble, had incurred no damage that was beyond repair. There had been no infidelity, no unbelieving spouse who had walked out. This was just two Christians who hadn't learned to think "we" instead of "me." They had never been taught to value and respect one another or nurture their love. Tragically, the biggest obstacle standing between them and reconciliation was Christian friends who kept fueling their frustrations and counseling them to give up. The very group of people who should have been cheering their efforts to save the marriage was threatening to sabotage the rescue mission.

At least part of this couple's problem was rooted in a misunderstanding of what marriage is all about. They, like most newlyweds today, saw marriage as a *contract,* which, according to my dictionary, is "a binding agreement." At the heart of every contract is a set of conditions or promises—the "deal." The deal is, you do this for me and I'll do that for you. A contract lays out what "this" and "that" consist of. It also has an escape clause, either stated or implied, which says that if you fail to do "this," then I can stop doing "that." And in recent times, quite frankly, many people don't feel that their contracts mean much of anything. All I need to justify breaking one is to say I'm not happy with the deal.

Tragically, this flexible concept of contracts is how many people now view marriage. "If my marriage is an ordeal," they say, "I'll opt out and look for a better deal somewhere else." This is the unspoken amendment many people attach to their spoken vows of matrimony. Men and women differ in a lot of ways when it comes to what they bring to the marriage relationship, but this is one weakness they both share. Thousands of husbands and wives exercise this escape clause every year.

A question well worth asking, then, if words have meaning and we desire to be responsible with our wedding vows, is the same question abbreviated on so many bracelets and other items in recent years: What would Jesus do? Or better yet, What would Jesus declare about marriage, divorce, and the meaning behind those vows so often heard at weddings? Wouldn't you know, Jesus essentially encountered this question with the Pharisees. We find this incident in the gospel of Matthew.

"Is it lawful for a man to divorce his wife for any reason at all?" (Matthew 19:3)

While the context here was the subject of divorce, the Pharisees' real intent was to trap Jesus. They were trying to undermine Him, to discredit Him publicly, and they knew that divorce was just the kind of issue to put Him on the hot seat. You see, some things never change. The people and their religious leaders were deeply divided over the issues surrounding divorce and remarriage. But why ask Him this particular question?

To find out, we need to do a little background check. During this time, there were two major schools of rabbis with entirely different perspectives on divorce. One school leaned heavily toward no. They said that a man could only divorce his wife if she committed adultery. The other school, which was more liberal, said that men could divorce their wives for any cause that displeased them. How heinous did the wife's offense have to be to warrant a divorce? Certain historical records say, essentially, that burning the toast at breakfast was enough. Jesus, though, responded differently to the Pharisees' question.

> *And He answered and said, "Have you not read that He who created them from the beginning made them male and female, and said, 'For this reason a man shall leave his father and mother and be joined to his wife, and the two shall become one flesh'?"* (Matthew 19:4–5)

Don't you love the wisdom of Jesus! He turned it right back on them and responded with His own question, which I'll paraphrase as, "Have you forgotten where marriage got its start . . . or what marriage is all about?" Jesus was telling them that if they really understood the origin of marriage, this debate would be over. To understand God's perspective on divorce, we must deepen our understanding of the meaning and nature of marriage.

Those of us who have made or are contemplating making marriage vows do well to contemplate and understand these words of Christ, because so much of our culture is confused about marriage. Just look at these ideas, which came from some kids when they were asked the simple question, "What, exactly, is marriage?"

> **Eric** (age six): Marriage is when you get to keep the girl and don't have to give her back to her parents.

> **Anita** (age nine): Marriage is when somebody has been dating for a while and the boy might propose to the girl, and he says to her, "I'll take you for my whole life, or at least until we have kids and get divorced."

That's a telling reply, isn't it? Perhaps most of us can identify with this little guy's response.

> **Will** (age seven): It gives me a headache just to think about this stuff! I'm just a kid. I don't need this kind of trouble!

Whether it's kids or adults, a whole lot of people today are confused about marriage and unaware of the nature of the vows they make at the altar. A growing number of young adults are so confused about or disillusioned by marriage that they, like young Will, just don't want to think about it. But the good news is that God has thought about it. A lot! Remember, it was His idea from the beginning. He knows us, He made us—both male and female —and He designed us for one another. And in Matthew 19 Jesus made clear that God has a purpose and a pattern for marriage. Verse 5 of Matthew 19 says it's to bring men and women together and verse 6 says that this union is to be permanent: "What therefore God has joined together, let no man separate."

That permanence is reflected in the covenant we make when we say "I do." Did you notice something? I didn't refer to marriage as a contract, but as a *covenant*. Some believe that covenant is just a spiritual word for contract, but it's not. The difference is real, and it can make a real difference in any marriage. It is the dimension of marriage to which we turn our attention now. We'll begin by reviewing the essence of marriage, to which Jesus alluded in the Matthew text. Then we'll then examine the covenant dimension of this unique relationship.

THE ESSENCE OF MARRIAGE: A REVIEW

What Jesus was doing when He responded to the Pharisees' question provides an ultracondensed review of the things we've been learning throughout this book. Continuing through verse 10 of Matthew 19, He gives us five points to ponder as we think about marriage. Before mentioning these points, I have to tell you about a couple in our church. Their names are Elsie and Jerry Heuer. And as I'm writing these words, their family and friends are planning a surprise anniversary party for them. Tomorrow, they'll celebrate seventy years together. No, this is not a misprint. Seventy years together and loving it!

Think about that for a moment. This couple got married just three months before the stock market crashed in 1929. Talk about a tough time to make a marriage work. But that's what they did . . . all through the Great Depression . . . all through the years of World War II . . . all through the growth years of the 1950s and the volatile years of the 1960s. Come to think of it, Jerry retired in 1964. I think I was in the fifth grade then. And today, these two

174

incredible people are still loving and serving one another and others. Whenever I wonder if love can last a lifetime, I think of Elsie and Jerry.

Back to the essence of marriage. Here are some crucial points to notice in Jesus' words to the Pharisees. It's as if Jesus takes them to school. Call it "Marriage 101."

In just seven verses Jesus lays down five essential components of God's blueprint for marriage.

- Marriage is custom-made by God.
- Marriage mysteriously unites two into one.
- Marriage is a solemn vow of allegiance.
- Marriage is a vow to God.
- Marriage is for life.

These five simple truths are radically different from the standards of our twenty-first century culture. Americans today view marriage as an arrangement designed by us, for us, for as long as we feel it's working. Where does Jesus get such a radically different view? Here's the text:

> *And He answered and said, "Have you not read that He who created them from the beginning made them male and female, and said, 'For this reason a man shall leave his father and mother and be joined to his wife, and the two shall become one flesh'? So they are no longer two, but one flesh. What therefore God has joined together, let no man separate." They said to Him, "Why then did Moses command to give her a certificate of divorce and send her away?" He said to them, "Because of your hardness of heart Moses permitted you to divorce your wives; but from the beginning it has not been this way. And I say to you, whoever divorces his wife, except for immorality, and marries another woman commits adultery."*
>
> *The disciples said to Him, "If the relationship of the man with his wife is like this, it is better not to marry." (Matthew 19:4–10)*

Lesson 1: Marriage is custom-made by our Creator for us. He did it "from the beginning," Jesus said in verse 4. He was saying that some things never change, and this one goes back all the way. It transcends every culture and generation on Planet Earth and in human history. From the very beginning, God designed this thing

175

called marriage for men and women to learn to live together and meet each other's needs. It's a great invention, but it takes work to keep it running smoothly. There is a tendency today to take God out of the picture altogether, to treat marriage as an invention of our culture. Perhaps, the rationale goes, like most great inventions, marriage as we traditionally think of it may have simply served its purpose, but it has failed to keep up with the times.

Although the forms can and should vary from generation to generation and culture to culture, the essence of marriage described by Jesus was, and is, not just a first-century Judeo-Christian tradition. It is rooted in the core values of God the Creator and the core needs of men and women of all time. And remember, we may be different by design, but God's master plan for marriage takes even our differences into account.

Lesson 2: In marriage, God mysteriously unites two into one. To me, this is the most amazing biblical truth about marriage. Jesus said, "They are no longer two, but one flesh." Many people think that this is speaking only about the sexual union between a woman and a man. That's definitely part of the marriage covenant, but there's a lot more to it. We see this in Jesus' word choice here. He said that the two will "be" one flesh. This marriage is not so much something two people *do*, but something they *become*. It's not just an act; it's a change of your condition. Think of it this way. The physical union of a man and woman is a beautiful gift from God. Jesus was reminding us that this gift, and all of life once we're married, is no longer about *me* and *you*. It's about *we* and *us*. That's a major difference. So when Becky and I, for example, talk and think about our marriage, we're working out what *we* think. Our individual thoughts and ideas massage each other to generate *our* ideas.

Another amazing thing that's underscored in Jesus' response is that marriage is not a human invention. "What therefore God has joined together" says that marriage is not something a man and woman do. It's not something Becky and I did in 1974. It's something God did when we came together and vowed our allegiance to one another and to God. It's almighty God who unites us, not the pastor or the ceremony, not the church or the state. You can see how our culture has lost sight of this fact by noticing the progression in the following dictionary definitions of marriage.

1828: A civil and religious contract instituted by God, binding on a man and a woman in marital fidelity until death.

1975: The state of being married or wedlock. An institution whereby men and women are joined in a special kind of social and legal dependence.

1991: An intimate living arrangement without legal sanction, a trial marriage, an intimate social engagement or union of any kind.

Quite a dramatic change in our culture's view of marriage, isn't it? From a binding contract (I prefer covenant) with Deity that remains in force until death to a humanly forged institution to a nonbinding living arrangement. Do you think that what goes through the mind of the average bride and groom when they stand at the altar has changed? Our culture has lost the powerful sense of mystery in a divine union. If men and women could only realize the importance of always thinking *we* instead of *me*, marriages would be revolutionized. In business terms, this is not about a new partnership but a complete merger. The two become one. No wonder Paul the apostle would later say to the Ephesians that the man "who loves his own wife loves himself" (Ephesians 5:28). It's true for the two of us.

Lesson 3: Marriage is a solemn vow of allegiance. Now we're getting to the core of Paul Sailhamer's insistence that words have meaning. Marriage is an unconditional covenant that you make with an imperfect person. Jesus made this clear when He said that a man is to "leave" his parents and "cleave" to his wife. Both of these words are packed with meaning. "Leave" is the Hebrew word *azab,* which means to loosen, relinquish, forsake, to leave utterly and totally. "Cleave" is the word *dabaq,* and it means to bond, glue, cling, adhere, be joined, stick, or fasten together. We're talking about the ultimate superglue here. It's the same word used in Deuteronomy 28:21 to describe how leprosy bonds to a person's skin. This is a permanent union.

The Bible often refers to this vow of allegiance as a covenant. Unlike a contract, which contains conditions that if unmet by the parties involved cause the contract to become null and void, a covenant is, by definition, unconditional. Granted, the full blessings of covenants may have conditions (see Psalm 103:17–18), but many covenants were unconditional commitments. And God's covenant with His people is unconditional. Although He may discipline them for a season, His love is never ending. "His lovingkindness (*hesed* in Hebrew) is everlasting," the repeated refrain of Psalm 136, is the rallying cry of *covenant*. Genesis 12:1–3 expresses God's covenant with Abraham and His people. It is a solemn, unconditional vow of allegiance.

Romans 11:2 declares that even though Israel strayed, God would not quit on them "whom He foreknew." He had chosen them and entered into a covenant-based love relationship with them. Therefore, He cannot, *will not,* abandon them. This "lovingkindness" at the heart of God's covenant with us should be the heart of our covenant as we wed.

The New Testament expression of grace—unmerited favor from God—is rooted in His covenant, unconditional love for us. Jesus referred to His blood in Matthew 26:28 as "My blood of the covenant," and in Luke 22:20 He declared that "this cup which is poured out for you is the new covenant in My blood." In other words, Christ's sacrifice on the cross guarantees that God's covenant promises to us will not go unfulfilled.

Covenants in the Old Testament world were often sealed or secured by a sacrifice. In Genesis 15, God reaffirmed His covenant to Abraham as he struggled with the fact that he and Sarah were childless. God reassured Abraham and had him prepare a sacrifice, which was to be cut in half and laid open in two opposite pieces. Then God Himself, as a flaming torch, passed between those two pieces. Often a covenant between two parties would be sealed by just such a sacrifice. The two parties would walk between the pieces of the sacrificed animal as a symbol of their commitment to fulfill their vows. The message behind this ceremony was powerful. They were saying, "May this be done to us if we forsake our covenant."

In passing through the sacrifice alone, God was guaranteeing, unconditionally, His promise to Abraham. Wow. What a statement of grace and allegiance to one's word!

The implications for our wedding vows, our covenant of marriage, are at once awesome, humbling, somewhat mystifying, and even terrifying. As we walk the aisle between our friends and family, we should turn and say to them, "If we ever show signs of breaking our vows, you let us have it!" More importantly, we then stand before God and say the same thing: "God, if I ever break these vows, You would be just to take my life." As we'll see in a moment, the only real audience that matters is an audience of One, the one true God, our Creator, Savior, and Lord—the Keeper of all covenants. Vows are a big deal, serious business, conducted in the very presence of God. But I'm getting ahead of myself. So let's go to our next lesson in Jesus' introductory course on marriage.

Lesson 4: Marriage is a vow to God as well as to one another. Listen to what one of God's prophets to Israel wrote when God's people were wondering why He seemed to have removed His blessing from them.

> *"This is another thing you do: you cover the altar of the Lord with tears, with weeping and with groaning, because He no longer regards the offering or accepts it with favor from your hand. Yet you say, 'For what reason?' Because the Lord has been a witness between you and the wife of your youth, against whom you have dealt treacherously, though she is your companion and your wife by covenant."* (Malachi 2:13–14)

Then the prophet summarized the reality of Israel's situation in verse 16:

> *"For I hate divorce," says the Lord, the God of Israel, "and him who covers his garment with wrong," says the Lord of hosts. "So take heed to your spirit, that you do not deal treacherously."*

The prophet was saying that God is the witness between a man and woman when they vow their allegiance to one another. Therefore the covenant is not only between those two people; it's also between them and God. And God's blessing may be removed whenever we neglect or "deal treacherously" with our spouse.

I don't think this principle applies only to divorce. It's linked in 1 Peter 3:7 to the quality of your marriage as well. Husbands, if you fail to "show her honor as a fellow heir of the grace of life," Peter said, your prayers may be hindered. Some of us think that we can deal lightly with our wives and have a heavy relationship with God, but it doesn't work that way. God wants us to make our marriages a priority and work on making them great, not just hang together with clenched teeth. This is why during a wedding I like to have couples look each other right in the eye when making their vows. This is serious business, not just legal pre-liminaries to the reception and honeymoon. Therefore, I'm proposing a new addition to the old tradition of exchanging vows. No, I'm not recommending split sacrifices instead of rose petals. After the couple has exchanged vows with each other, they should turn and look upward or bow their heads in prayer or maybe approach an empty chair (representing the real but unseen presence of God), and talk directly to their Lord as they repeat their vows to the Lord of the covenant. He is, after all, the most important Guest, the Audience to whom we will ultimately be accountable. And remember, He is the One who now joins the two into one. But I'm ahead of myself again. Let's move on to a final lesson.

Lesson 5: Marriage is for life. "Let no man separate" what God has joined together, Jesus said, but today more couples divorce than remain married. And while Malachi said that God hates divorce, a recent study at the University of Minnesota estimates that this year (2000) about 60 percent of marriages will fail. Jesus' stand would obviously frustrate many in twenty-first-century American culture, and apparently it frustrated the Pharisees too. That seems evident by the fact that since He answered their first question—"Is it lawful for a man to divorce his wife for any reason at all?"—with a question, they asked Him another one.

"Why then did Moses command to give her a certificate of divorce and send her away?" (Matthew 19:7)

It's as if they were challenging Jesus. "Hey, Lord," is the tone of their question, "it sounds like You're teaching that there's no divorce. Then why did Moses command that we give her a certificate and divorce her?" They were quoting from the Old Testament book of Leviticus. His response is incredibly instructive.

"Because of your hardness of heart Moses permitted you to divorce your wives; but from the beginning it has not been this way." (Matthew 19:8)

The pivotal word in Jesus' statement is *permitted*. Moses never commanded anyone to divorce; he only granted permission. Big difference. This is, I believe, consistent with the rest of Scripture.

Under very limited circumstances God permits divorce. Jesus identified these circumstances in the rest of His reply.

> *"And I say to you, whoever divorces his wife, except for immorality, and marries another woman commits adultery."* (Matthew 19:9)

These are tough words to hear in our culture, aren't they? Many of us don't think this way. We like Jesus' views on other topics, but not this one.

The problem here, Jesus said, is our hardened hearts. That's what messes up marriages. If our hearts were soft to God, I believe any two people could make a great marriage. Not just a *good* marriage, but a *great* one. It takes two soft hearts willing to listen to God, to change and be molded and obedient to His Word. Even in cases involving immorality, cases where Jesus said divorce is permitted, it's important to remind ourselves that it is not commanded.

I have been amazed over my years in pastoral ministry at the number of couples who have weathered the tragedy of infidelity and rebuilt their marriages because of a willingness to repent and forgive. Infidelity has tragic, painful consequences that produce deep wounds and leave nasty scars. But by grace these wounds can heal and the scars can, with time, fade. They may never completely disappear; but just as many people can learn to live with physical scars, slowly ceasing to notice them or be bothered by them, so it is with the emotional scars of unfaithfulness.

Interestingly, forgiveness is what Jesus taught about leading up to Matthew 19. In fact, the last two lessons Jesus gave before this discussion in Matthew 19 of marriage, divorce, and infidelity are (1) the importance of lovingly *confronting sin* in God's family (Matthew 18:15–20); and (2) the *imperative to forgive* as we've been forgiven (Matthew 18:21–35). I can't believe that the order is just a coincidence. What a difference it would make if we, the church, could apply both of these skills to help heal wounded relationships. Friends who confront the early signs of an affair—vulnerability, inappropriateness, flirting, or downright risky relationships with the opposite sex—may well prevent the affair from ever happening. Confronting and forgiving are two of the basics for building strong marriages.

We're to forgive "seventy times seven," Jesus told Peter. The implication is that unlimited forgiveness is the standard. This hard teaching on forgiveness certainly relates to Jesus' discussion about divorce. Jesus made it clear that forgiveness and restoration are His desire, because marriage was designed from the start to be a covenant relationship, a lifetime commitment.

At this point you may be thinking, *Now, wait a minute, Dale. What if I'm already divorced? What do I do?* I want to leave you with three words, but first, we need to mention what I think the Bible says are some other cases where divorce is permitted. One is the case of desertion of a Christian spouse by a non-Christian partner. In 1 Corinthians 7:10–16, the apostle Paul discussed a different scenario than the one Jesus addressed.

> *But to the married I give instructions, not I, but the Lord, that the wife should not leave her husband (but if she does leave, she must remain unmarried, or else be reconciled to her husband), and that the husband should not divorce his wife.*
>
> *But to the rest I say, not the Lord, that if any brother has a wife who is an unbeliever, and she consents to live with him, he must not divorce her. And a woman who has an unbelieving husband, and he consents to live with her, she must not send her husband away. For the unbelieving husband is sanctified through his wife, and the unbelieving wife is sanctified through her believing husband; for otherwise your children are unclean, but now they are holy. Yet if the unbelieving one leaves, let him leave; the brother or the sister is not under bondage in such cases, but God has called us to peace. For how do you know, O wife, whether you will save your husband? Or how do you know, O husband, whether you will save your wife?*

Paul addressed the case of a believer's being left, abandoned, or divorced by an unbeliever. Notice even here that the heart of God is for the marriage covenant to be honored. The marriage, even to an unbeliever, is to be maintained, not severed, if at all possible. In fact, it can hopefully lead to the salvation of the lost spouse if he or she experiences the blessing of living under the same roof as one of God's beloved children. (Note that the reference to being "sanctified" through the believing wife or husband cannot mean "saved" but merely "set apart," "sacred," or "holy" by virtue of being identified with or sharing a home and family with a believing spouse.)

For the purpose of our topic, however, note that 1 Corinthians 7:15 declares that the abandoned spouse is "not under bondage." In the Greek text, this is strong language implying true release from the relationship. There is much more to be said about this issue. It is not, however, my intent in this book to explore all the complexities of it, but merely to acknowledge those complexities.

Cases such as abuse of the spouse or children, abandonment, and sexual addiction are also dreadfully destructive to a marriage. Deciding exactly when divorce should be permitted in such cases is one of the most difficult challenges faced by theologians, pastors, and counselors. It calls for the wisdom of Solomon, the courage of Joshua, and the compassion of Hosea all at the same time. Few of us, if we are honest, possess even one of those traits, let alone all three at the same time. For a more thorough study of the various perspectives on divorce and remarriage, I would suggest such books as *Divorce and Remarriage* by Guy Duty or *The Divorce Decision* by Gary Richmond.[1]

Again, while divorce *may* be permitted in some of these instances, always remember that God's first choice would be forgiveness and restoration. And after reading the Scriptures, no matter what view you hold on these issues, don't miss the main points in Jesus' teaching on marriage:

1. Marriage is designed by God to be a lifelong covenant.
2. When that covenant is threatened, for any reason, it breaks the heart of God.
3. When you are hurting, lead with honest confrontation and forgiveness.

Above all, pray for your heart and the heart of your spouse to be softened. Because in the end, it's the hardness of our hearts that leads to the heartache and heartbreak of divorce that devastates countless couples.

OK, now the three words. If you're already divorced, *repent, repair,* and *restart.*

First, face your sin honestly and *repent* of it. If the divorce was outside of God's will, be honest, admit it, and claim His grace. In most cases, no matter who initiated the divorce, no matter which spouse was the primary cause, we all need to face whatever sin contributed to the struggle and breakdown of the relationship. Be honest and ask God to show you what your next step should be.

Second, *repair* by seeking forgiveness and restoration with the Lord and with your former partner if at all possible. If you now know that your divorce was outside God's will, see if the marriage can be repaired and restored. There is hope. I've seen it happen. Even if the marriage cannot be salvaged, then seek to repair any areas of your life that may have contributed to the breakdown. If you don't, you will carry those flaws into any future relationships.

Finally, *restart* by doing what Jesus said: "Go and sin no more" (see John 5:14; 8:11). Don't repeat the mistake. God's grace is available. Divorce is forgivable, but don't abuse God's grace. Don't spend the rest of your life beating yourself for past sins. Christ was beaten for you and your sins. A great verse for the restart is Philippians 3:12. Listen to it:

> *Not that I have already obtained it or have already become perfect, but I press on so that I may lay hold of that for which also I was laid hold of by Christ Jesus.*

Let the Cross free you to go—repentant, repaired, and ready to represent Jesus—to a world of other wounded people. God can use you if you let Him.

MARRIAGE AS A LIFELONG COVENANT: AN ESSENTIAL FOR SUCCESS

When I reflect on Jesus' words to the Pharisees, I'm encouraged. But that's not the reaction of the disciples who were listening to Jesus lay it out for the Pharisees. They heard it loud and clear that marriage is for keeps, designed for the long haul. Listen to their reaction:

> *The disciples said to Him, "If the relationship of the man with his wife is like this, it is better not to marry." (Matthew 19:10)*

As men often do, they got part of the lesson, but missed the big idea. They saw these stricter guidelines against divorce as a trap to be avoided. Since you can never really know if you'll be happy, and since you can't get out for "any old reason," then let's form a new Christian club for bachelors! But that's certainly not God's reason for the lifelong covenant commitment called marriage. God knows that the marriage covenant is not a trap for failure. It's a tool for lifelong success. Once we grasp that divine perspective, God begins to change the way we *think* about our marriages. I can identify five areas in which our thinking needs to be transformed if we are to achieve a fulfilling marriage.

- Think God
- Think Team
- Think Long-term
- Think Commitment

Think God. Keep Him in the center of your marriage. Why? If I think about God, I realize that the covenant I made at the altar was with Him as well as with Becky. When I keep that in mind, I realize that through Christ on the cross God provided the *model* of how to love my wife. He is my *Mentor* for forgiveness. He modeled how to forgive her when she fails and how she can forgive me when I fail. God is also my *motivation* to persevere. If Becky is having a bad day, she may not be too loveable. I know there are plenty of times when I'm not very loveable. But our covenant says we're going to love each other anyway. That covenant is with God too, and when we look in His face, He always looks good. Ultimately, our motivation is to please Him. Think God as your model, Mentor, and motivation to carry on.

Think team. Recognizing marriage as a lifelong commitment makes me realize that we win or lose together, which boosts my motivation to make our marriage a winner. Since the marriage covenant is a lifelong commitment, my only other alternative is to live in misery my whole life, and who wants that? Not me. When I think *team,* my motivation to avoid divorce increases as well, because there are no winners in divorce. Even when I'm angry, tired, or frustrated, I remember that it's about *us,* not just *me.* We are in this thing *together.* So I'd best invest in my greatest asset, my wife.

Think long-term. To do so helps me go through the seasonal ups and downs, the swings in our level of marital satisfaction.

Marriage is a lot like the stock market. One day, whew, it's up 200 points. I'm ready to sign up for two lifetimes. Other days, the market goes pretty low. I want to sell. But if you're in the stock market, is it smart to sell every time the market drops? Of course not. Seasoned investors say to hang in there, because over the long haul you'll come out ahead. But selling out is exactly what many people do in marriage. When it drops, they bail out. That's a bad decision with your stocks; it's a worse decision with your marriage. Stick with it for the long haul.

Think investment. Let's stick with that financial analogy. Investing in your marriage means you realize that even small investments, small sacrifices, deposited consistently over time, produce great dividends. A friend of mine, a financial advisor, points out that saving merely $1 per day from age twenty-one until retirement, assuming an average interest rate of just 7 percent, will result in about a million dollars at age sixty-five. Wow. Marriage investments are just like that, only better! You can have a million-dollar marriage long before retirement because the dividends are far greater. I love the way J. Allan Petersen put it.

> Most people come to marriage believing it is a box full of goodies from which we extract all we need to make us happy. . . .
> Marriage is an empty box. There's nothing in it. It is an opportunity to put something in, to do something for marriage. Marriage was never intended to do something for anybody. People are expected to do something for marriage. If you do not put into the box more than you take out, it becomes empty. Love isn't in marriage, it is in people, and people put it into marriage. Romance, consideration, generosity aren't in marriage, they are in people, and people put them into the marriage box. . . .
> Living for each other releases both of you to relax your grip and work together productively to keep the box full.[2]

Think commitment—and communicate it consistently. Reaffirming your love and loyalty for life actually enhances the quality of your relationship. Why? *First, security is the key to honesty.* If I don't think my marriage is secure, guess what? I'm going to hold my cards close to the vest. I'm not going to reveal what I really think and feel, because if I tell the truth, maybe my spouse will leave me. *Second, honesty is the key to intimacy.* Without honesty in our relationship, we can never develop intimacy. But when we're able to be honest with each other, we draw closer together in every area of our life. *Finally, intimacy is the key to joy.* With intimacy comes a deep sense of security, and joy flourishes in that sort of environment. Threats of leaving will never strengthen your marriage. But responding to moments of vulnerability or even anger with assurances of your commitment will deepen your love on every level.

Imagine, for example, that you're exasperated and you say to your spouse, "Honey, right now I'm so angry, but I'm going to love you for life whether you like it or not. So let's go to work on this thing, because I want to make you the happiest person on earth. It's obvious I'm not doing that right now, but I committed to never stop trying. Please help me." Believe me, the kind of attitude reflected in a statement like that will go a long way toward revitalizing any marriage.

Remember Jerry and Elsie Heuer. Listen to their son Ken's reflections on the depth of their commitment and its impact on their lives and the lives of those they loved.

This summer my parents celebrated seventy years of marriage. They were honored by their children, grandchildren, and great-grandchildren. To all of us, they have been an unequaled example of what God expects from us when we make a covenant. As I reflect over the scores of years they have been together, I have so many memories. I remember them taking in four of my cousins when my aunt died. I was in high school and the cousins were all younger than me. To this day those cousins still look to my mom and dad as their own. During the time my cousins were with us, Mom and Dad worked as a team to care for us all. I'm sure there was plenty of stress for them, but we never knew it. Through the years their home has served as a safe haven for many relatives and friends, including a great-uncle and my grandparents. Love always abounded. If ever there was a time that their vows were challenged, it never was visible to anyone around them. I really believe that their commitment to each other was strong at the time of their marriage, and as they walked with the Lord their promises to each other grew consistently deeper and richer.

Amen.

NOTES

1. Guy Duty, *Divorce and Remarriage* (Minneapolis: Bethany House, 1967); Gary Richmond, *The Divorce Decision* (Waco, Tex.: Word, 1988).
2. J. Allan Petersen, *The Myth of the Greener Grass* (Wheaton, Ill.: Tyndale, 1991), 182–85.

CHAPTER TEN

LOVE AND MARRIAGE

Basically, biologically and, most importantly, biblically, women and men are different by design for good reason. We've spent nine chapters looking at these differences from God's perspective, seeking to better understand how they can work together to create harmony in a marriage. But as different as men and women may be, whether we're from Mars or Venus or any other sphere in the universe, we share one final universal need—love. Poets cry for it and songwriters celebrate it.

Most would agree that without love, life becomes unlivable. A common complaint in the divorce courts of America is "Our love just seemed to die." Without love, it's hard to imagine that any of us could pull off the first nine chapters of this book or any other manual on marriage. The fact that loving is indeed foundational to living came through crystal clear in Jesus' teaching. He placed it at the top of all the commandments.

> "'You shall love the Lord your God with all your heart, and with all your soul, and with all your mind.' This is the great and foremost commandment. The second is like it, 'You shall love your neighbor as yourself.'" (Matthew 22:37–39)

What I'm hearing Jesus say is that loving is at the heart of living together. That's the core message of His great commandment. "Love God and love people" is the abridged version of it. Which means all that we've learned from the Bible about the differences between men and women, all the biblical commands, all the wisdom of God's Word will be wasted on us if we don't master the art of loving. Love and marriage really do go together like the proverbial horse and carriage. Without love, marriage is going nowhere.

So what does God have to say about love? Plenty, and the most profound yet practical insights are undoubtedly found in the thirteenth chapter of Paul's first letter to the Corinthian church. You know it as the text that's so often read at marriage ceremonies. But while we're all familiar with the middle verses of that chapter—love is patient, love is kind, and so forth—listen to the first three verses.

> *If I speak with the tongues of men and of angels, but do not have love, I have become a noisy gong or a clanging cymbal. If I have the gift of prophecy, and know all mysteries and all knowledge; and if I have all faith, so as to remove mountains, but do not have love, I am nothing. And if I give all my possessions to feed the poor, and if I surrender my body to be burned, but do not have love, it profits me nothing.* (1 Corinthians 13:1–3)

As I read these lines, I'm tempted to substitute some concepts that we've covered in this book, because the principles Paul outlined apply so appropriately to love and marriage.

ULTIMATE COMMUNICATION, DIVORCED OF LOVE, IS WORTHLESS

For example, doesn't the line "If I speak with the tongues of men and of angels" address communication, which we discussed in chapters 4 through 6? According to Paul, the result of this sort of communication, this speaking "with the tongues of men and of angels," minus love, is noise. Nothing but noise. How about if I understand everything about communication in this book and apply all the principles that have been covered, "but do not have love"? What can I expect? I'll probably hammer my spouse, like a percussionist raps on a cymbal with his drumstick to make it clang. Which means that without love I have nothing of value to say. Nothing worth listening to. In fact, I'm likely to use my slick communication skills to harm or manipulate instead of heal or minister.

I'll never forget the time Tim (not his real name) and his young bride Jill came in for some pastoral counseling. To the casual observer, they looked like the all-American couple. You know, beautiful people, always happy, full of smiles and laughter after church or in front of their neighbors. But as they began to talk with me, a pattern quickly developed.

Tim began by explaining that they just needed a little help and were really very happy overall. He even apologized for taking up my valuable time. He told me how he felt, what he thought, and what he planned to do. This guy was quite the talker. He was verbally gifted and happy to display that talent. I finally caught him taking a breath and interrupted. "Now, Jill, how are you doing?" I asked. She hesitated, as if afraid to speak. Her eyes glanced at Tim as if to say, "Can I really be honest here?" Then, just as her lips parted, Tim jumped in again. "Jill would tell you that she feels . . . she thinks . . . she wants . . ." He gave me the complete lowdown on his wife.

So I tried again. "Jill, now tell me how you see all of this." Again, she hesitated and Tim launched into his speech, but this time I stopped him. "Time-out," I said. "Tim, I really want to hear Jill speak for herself." I thought I might have to get my duct tape to keep him from taking over again!

Tim was a great communicator but a lousy lover. It was only after Jill spoke for herself that he found out what was really in the mind of his wife. And she gave him a giant piece of her mind that day, a gift that was long overdue.

ULTIMATE KNOWLEDGE, DIVORCED OF LOVE, IS USELESS

Let's try another line. "If I . . . know all mysteries and all knowledge." Unraveled mysteries are what we've been focusing on in the previous nine chapters. The mysterious differences between women and men. And *knowledge* is our understanding of this particular topic. But if I gain these things "but do not have love, I am nothing." Isn't that ironic? We'd expect that if we gained mastery of a topic like marriage we'd automatically have something to contribute. We might consider ourselves qualified to teach classes or seminars. Maybe even get a little bit uppity about our level of expertise. But the Bible declares that if we gain all this head knowledge, and even factor in a modicum of faith, but do it without love, we are nothing. Those are strong words there. It doesn't even say we're mediocre. It says we are *nothing* if we amass all this knowledge with a loveless attitude. One thing's for certain: If I get all these principles about how a marriage is supposed to look and don't let love guide my application of them, I'm bound to develop serious problems at home.

A well-known pastor who spoke and wrote frequently on the topic of marriage comes to mind. This guy had plenty of knowledge, plenty of answers to people's questions about marriage. Yes, he knew more about marriage than I'll ever know. He could do a series of books on the topic. But he had failed to apply his great "wisdom" in his own home. His own love relationship had dried up and he adopted a hidden, secret life of adultery and infidelity. He was a great teacher of theory, but a failure at loving his own wife. What a chilling reminder that we face serious challenges when we get serious about blending our differences as men and women into a single relationship.

ULTIMATE SACRIFICE, DIVORCED OF LOVE, STILL DISAPPOINTS GOD

How about one more line? "If I give all my possessions to feed the poor, and . . . surrender my body to be burned." Sounds like the apostle was talking about serving others, doesn't it? I'd say *sacrificial service,* in fact, judging by his word choice. Done without love, though, ultimate service is doomed to the same fate as great communication and a genius IQ applied in a world without love. "It profits me nothing." This is one area where, unfortunately, folks in full-time ministry, such as pastors, can be the best illustrations. I've known plenty of people, particularly pastors, who were great at serving every conceivable person, meeting every identifiable need in the church, but at the expense of their relationship with their own wives and children.

Believe me, this is an easy trap to fall into. I fell into it early in my marriage and ministry. Becky and I were young parents of two toddlers and were pastoring our first church out of seminary. Summer was in full swing as we headed off to our week-long youth camp. The setting was a beautiful, secluded island on a lake in Tennessee. By secluded I mean primitive, without any electricity or running water. Picture Gilligan's Island without the professor or Maryanne—or anyone else for that matter. And yes, I was pretty much cut from the same cloth as Gilligan when it came to fixing things. We were roughing it. So as we landed on the island and hauled everything ashore, I kicked into servant mode and set about helping all the kids from church get their tents pitched and campsites set up. I was even helping kids gather wood and cook their food, which struck me as especially servantlike because I so seldom do that at home.

Meanwhile, Becky was doing her best to set up our campsite, set up a makeshift kitchen, help kids find their misplaced gear, all while trying to keep Beth, our toddler, from heading off to the lake and Paul, our crawler, from eating handfuls of dirt or shale. If my memory serves me correctly, she was just about on her last nerve when I poked my head in our tent and said something incredibly insensitive like, "Hey, sweetheart, isn't this great? We're going to have a fantastic week here with these kids!"

"You're going to have a fantastic week," was how her reply started, "because I'm taking the kids and going back home."

"What? What's wrong?" Of course I was clueless and therefore baffled.

"I haven't seen you since we landed on this island," she explained.

"Well, that's because I've been helping all these kids get settled in. After all, this is my job," I defended.

"If you would have paid just a little attention, you would have seen that I've been doing the same thing, plus trying to keep track of Beth and Paul. If this is how it's going to be for the week, then I'll just go home and take care of the kids by myself there."

At this point, you'll be pleased to know, I got the picture, apologized for my insensitivity, and started shouldering my share of the child care and Burke campsite load. We did end up having a great week, and in addition to the lessons I taught the youth around the campfire each night, I went home having learned an important lesson myself. If my service is at the expense of loving my wife, "it profits me nothing."

So what's the point of verses 1–3? Even if I possess the best communication skills, even if I hold three Ph.D.'s in the field of interpersonal relationships, even if I do all the right things for my spouse, showering him or her with gifts, all my words, insights, and actions are worthless without love. That's why Jesus put love at the top of His "must do" list as the greatest commandment. So what is this mysterious, unifying thing called *love*? In the next four verses, the God who made us so different defined it for us.

SO WHAT IS LOVE, ANYHOW?

I think you get the picture that love, godly love, is essential for a marriage to work. But what does that kind of love look like? Fortunately, Paul put it in terms we can understand.

Love is patient, love is kind and is not jealous; love does not brag and is not arrogant, does not act unbecomingly; it does not seek its own, is not provoked, does not take into account a wrong suffered, does not rejoice in unrighteousness, but rejoices with the truth; bears all things, believes all things, hopes all things, endures all things. (1 Corinthians 13:4–7)

Each one of Paul's "love is" statements represents a different facet of the only kind of love that one can confidently characterize as a love that truly "never fails," which he said in verse 8. As much as I appreciate a good, insightful book on relationships, when all is said and done, it is *love* that never fails. The best of principles are only as good as the love that backs them up. But society today is often confused and conflicted about what love really is. We've all been fooled by someone we thought "loved" us. Then we learned the meaning behind the familiar question, "With friends like that, who needs enemies?"

But 1 Corinthians 13 breaks love into fourteen bite-sized pieces so we can get a taste of the real thing. A dozen plus two words or phrases that flesh out this eternal, mystical concept called love. So let's take a moment to consider each one.

Love is patient. The patience described here reflects that *love waits with contentment.* It means I wait without demanding change. I wait without anxiety. I wait without anger. This patience is more than either an attitude or an action. It's an action with

an attitude. One writer said that patience is faith waiting for a nib-
ble. I can relate to that. If I'm sitting in my little fishing boat and
I have faith that there really are some keepers below the waterline,
I'll sit under that hot summer sun all day long waiting for one to
bite. That's patience.

The difference between us as husbands and wives, or just as
two human beings uniquely created by the Master Designer, absolutely demands patience. I'd like to produce a bumper sticker
that declares, "Waiting Happens." It is a fact of life that crossing
the wilderness would have taken the nation of Israel half the time
if it were an all-male entourage. Just getting packed is an experience that demands that I love my wife Becky by being patient,
waiting with an attitude of contentment. For me—and most
guys—it's purely mathematics. Three-day trip? Three pairs of
socks, three shirts, three pairs of underwear and one pair of jeans,
khakis, or shorts that match all the shirts. Elapsed time: fifteen
minutes if distracted by ESPN while packing.

But our wives are different. The bed is soon covered with
stacks, sorted and color coded for endless possibilities that I could
never even *imagine,* let alone plan for. I used to get impatient
with Becky until it hit me what was going on. Men pack clothes.
Women pack choices. And choices matter to women more than
men. So men, love your wives by being patient . . . and offer them
your unused half of the suitcase without some snide remark about
needing a trunk or trailer for the trip.

Of course, Becky needs to love me with patience too. I have a
habit of waiting until everyone's in the car, ready to go, and then
remembering that I need to check the oil. This tests Becky's patience
because the entire rest of the year I never check the oil. But years
ago I watched my dad, right before leaving on trips, always checking the oil. It's a ritual that must be performed for the trip to qualify as a genuine family adventure. So, ladies, remember, love waits
with joy while her husband checks the oil. Love is patient.

Love is kind. Paul linked patience and kindness for good reason. Just as two candles shed more light than one in the dark-
ness, so patience and kindness together tend to speak the message
of love more forcefully, without any need for words. Kindness has
been called the only universal language. Even those who cannot
communicate verbally can speak it, and those who are hearing im-
paired can hear and understand it. The reason is simple. Kind-

ness is first and foremost an action. It is love expressed by what we do. With this in mind, we can take this as a valid definition of kindness: *Love sees a need and meets it.*

I love when I respond and take the initiative to help wherever needed. When I think of love that's kind, I think of all those old *Superman* episodes I watched as a kid. Just when Lois Lane, little Jimmy, or some innocent citizen of Metropolis was in a fix, swoosh . . . "Look, up in the sky. It's bird, it's a plane, it's . . . Superman!" At the heart of the man with a big S on his chest was a kind spirit. Never hurtful, always helpful. The fact is, you don't need to be faster than a speeding bullet, more powerful than a locomotive, or able to leap tall buildings in a single bound to be kind. Just see a need and meet it. Help out. Lend a hand. And when you swoosh in when your husband or wife least expects it, its effectiveness as an expression of love doubles or even triples. Random acts of kindness, swift and unexpected, are a great way to surprise one another with love.

But beware, we are different by design. Remember, see a need and meet it, but make sure your spouse wants to be helped. Ladies, too much unsolicited "kindness" can feel like mothering to a man. Every man was designed by God to have one mother and one wife. Not two mothers. But, you men, though, with most wives, can't miss with kindness. Just make sure your helping always conveys love and never a spirit of mistrust.

Love is not jealous. At the root of jealousy is a burning desire to have what I cannot or do not have. And if I can't get it one way, I'll try another and another and another until I get what I want. If I have to go to war, so be it. Jealousy is all about possession and control. But this is the classic case of winning a battle but losing the war. The jealous husband or wife may win control in the short run, but a spirit of mistrust will do little to endear the "possessed" to the "possessor." People are not possessions to be owned, put in their place and controlled. Love doesn't seek to control; it trusts and grants freedom. What Paul meant when he said that love is not jealous is this: *Love trusts instead of controls.*

When he wrote that love is not jealous, it's possible that he had something else, or something more in mind than mere jealousy. The Greek word he used can also mean "envious," hence the *New International Version*'s translation of this verse: "Love . . . does not envy." This is similar to not being jealous in two ways. First, it involves a choice. Second, it brings freedom. When I reject jealousy, I choose to trust my spouse. When I reject envy, I choose to trust God. And great freedom comes when love chooses to remove envy from the equation, because suddenly I'm free to celebrate and enjoy not only my successes but also my spouse. I'm content. I don't want anyone else, and I pour my affections on that special gift God has given me in marriage. So when you think of a love that is not envious, think of it like this: *Love trusts God and is content with what He gives.*

Beware of both envy and jealousy. Replace them with contentment, trust, and freedom. Jealousy and mistrust will smother the romance in a marriage, so give it up. When you choose, and it is a choice, to "drink water from your own cistern" (Proverbs 5:15) and to "rejoice in the wife (or husband) of your youth" (Proverbs 5:18), love comes alive.

Love does not brag. When it comes to marriage, arrogance may win a battle, but it will never make you a champion lover. And if you're serious about going the distance in your marriage, the attitude of arrogance that's reflected in boastful language will never win you points with either your spouse or your Savior. Servant-hearted lovers simply aren't into arrogance. When it comes to love that doesn't brag, then, here's a definition that wins the day: *Love speaks of others more than itself.*

One of the greatest ways to freshen up a marriage is to brag on the strengths of your husband or wife. Not in an artificial or condescending way, but as the natural expression of your admiration. Let's face it, when someone builds you up publicly, despite the initial awkwardness, it makes you feel great inside. As much as we're inclined toward humility, we all like it when our spouse compliments us in front of others. Besides, it's pretty hard to brag when you're passing along well-deserved words of praise about those you love, especially your husband or wife.

I love to watch a woman when her husband brags on her. She may look downward, as if embarrassed, but I guarantee you she is beaming inside. Like the Proverbs 31 woman, she enjoys being praised "in the gates" by her husband. It is good for her children to "rise up and call her blessed." Men, if you want to turn on your wife in private, try turning up your praise in public. A final tip, men: This too is doubled in effectiveness when you brag not just to your guy friends but to your wife's friends.

Ladies, admiration expressed publicly for your husband is a great gift of love that men enjoy as well as, maybe even *more* than, you do. It is a powerful expression of respect and, as we saw earlier, men feel loved when they're respected. Ephesians 5:33 sums it up. "The wife must see to it that she respects her husband."

Love is not arrogant. Arrogance is the attitude behind the words of the boaster. When arrogance shows up, love soon disappears. Arrogance and its companion, pride, have an overinflated sense of their own importance. They demand to be the center of attention. They are puffed up. Hence our definition for not being arrogant: *Love stays humble, inflating others instead of itself.* A spirit of humility is the inverse of arrogance. People who stay humble, no matter what measure of success they attain or position of power they hold, can be potent lovers of others. An arrogant spirit will smother any expression of love, but a humble heart overflows with acts of love without even trying.

As we saw in chapters 4–6 of this book, God's master plan for the roles of husbands and wives is constructed on a foundation of servanthood. Our focus, like the focus of the waiter on his customers in a fine restaurant, must be on our spouse. We are to serve one another. Love does just that. It tunes its antennae (as damaged as they may be from the Fall) to our spouses instead of to ourselves. Humility, like the "seek" function on my car's radio, will keep on looking until it picks up the signal. But the arrogant husband or wife will be an impotent lover since all his or her affection is tuned in and concerned with one favorite station: WMMM. The voice of Me, Me, Me.

Love does not act unbecomingly. Bragging and arrogance are two examples of undesirable or unbecoming behavior, but there are plenty more. We call many of these behaviors bad manners, which prompts a practical definition for love that does not act unbecomingly: *Love has good manners.* Good manners should really be in every spouse's job description. They are expressed in countless ways, but five basic ones come to mind, all of which communicate the same message—I love you! They are:

1. Say, "Please." "Gimme, gimme" is not in the servant-lover's vocabulary. In the context of marriage, it's a shame that we drop this common courtesy from our requests. Say it and mean it and see what happens. You'll be pleasantly surprised.

2. Say, "Thank you." It's the quickest way to say you value another person. Men and women feel loved when they feel ap-
   preciated. When "Thank you" is accompanied by a "sneak
   attack," like a hug when they least expect it, the love potential goes up exponentially.
3. Say, "Excuse me" or "I'm sorry." This reinforces the idea
   that I have no right to interrupt, to bully my way into your
   world, to dominate your agenda, or to "bump" into your
   conversation.
4. Ask, "Can I help you?" Use of this endangered phrase carries with it the element of surprise that qualifies it as a random act of kindness. Warning: Guys, your wives have a
   tendency to say "No, thanks" even when they'd love to have
   some help, so just do it. And when she says, "You don't *need*
   to do that," just respond, "I know I don't need to; I just
   want to be here with you." She'll probably think you have
   ulterior motives, but she'll still love it.
5. Say, "You go first." No display of manners is more loving,
   or more Christian, than this one. Jesus said, "Many who
   are first will be last," and "The greatest among you shall
   be your servant." Men, our wives still love to have doors
   opened for them, not because they are weak, but because
   they are special.

Love does not seek its own. Love gets people's attention because it sticks out in the crowd. Such is the case with this unique
trait. A more literal rendering might be "Love does not seek to further its own profit or advantage." Blunt English translation: *Love
is not selfish.* When he wrote to the church at Philippi, the term
Paul used to describe one who loves this way was *servant,* and it
provided an ideal definition for this attribute of love. Love that
does not seek its own means: *Love has a servant spirit.* This is
not just a passive process, but an active one. It's not just sitting
back and letting others go first; it's lifting others up, escorting them
to the front of the line.

I believe that if I had to choose one phrase for love in
1 Corinthians 13, it would be this attribute. In a way, all the others are expressed in the image of love as a servant. The true servant has only one agenda: the Master's. As a servant, a husband
or wife must be patient and kind and never jealous or envious.

They certainly shouldn't be arrogant or braggadocian. A worthy servant exercises good manners, never flies off the handle in anger (especially toward the Master), and can't afford to keep records of wrongs. A great servant lives righteously, speaks honestly, and perseveres tenaciously until the job is done. The servant-lover is a great image that fits any wallet or purse and is worthy of being framed and hung in every room of the house.

Love is not provoked. To be provoked means to let another person's words or actions rouse or incite you to anger. Serious anger. Violent and vindictive anger. Savory anger you're unwilling to release. To prevent that from happening, you need a definition like this for love that is not provoked: *Love has a slow fuse.* At no time is a slow fuse more of an asset than when we get upset. Anger is one of our trickier emotions. Sometimes when we feel angry we try to convince ourselves that it's no big deal—that Christians shouldn't let such silly things bother them. Just ignore anger and it'll go away. Don't believe it. With human beings, anger is part of every relationship and must be processed. It is a menace that continually threatens. To deny that threat is like swimming among sharks with an open wound on your foot. Eventually, you will feel the bite!

In marriage, think of bitterness or anger as nasty weeds in your garden. Weeds and anger have a lot in common. They both

- start below the surface;
- seem harmless when they're small;
- often have deep roots that are hard to remove;
- do not die easily;
- multiply rapidly; and
- are invasive, spreading to other areas.

But love is a great preventative. It is slow to allow the seeds of bitterness to take root. If they do, and anger comes to full bloom (or should I say, full "boom"?), love searches out the root of the problem and is quick to forgive. That leads us to the next two qualities of real love.

Love does not take into account a wrong suffered. It is easier to say "love is not provoked" than to do it, and unforgiveness is one huge reason for this difficulty. Our definition, then, for love that does not take into account a wrong suffered is brief: *Love for-*

gives. Let's face it. Most of us struggle with forgiveness. We live to get even. Keeping short accounts—even *no* accounts—of wrongs done against us can be a daunting assignment. There is no way we can address this crucial element of love in a few short lines. So, if this is your biggest challenge, go back to chapter 7.

As a reminder, though, remember that there are two elements to forgiveness. One is *mercy,* which simply means not giving someone what he *does* deserve. This doesn't mean a reciprocal response isn't warranted. Our sense of justice may scream for it. But no marriage is built on justice. The marriage of any imperfect man to a less-than-perfect woman must be built on mercy and grace, not justice and revenge. But when we hold back our bitterness and wrath, when we choose to not punish, we're giving mercy. God showed us mercy when we deserved to die for our sin, but He sent Jesus to pay that price for us instead.

The second element of this forgiveness is *grace,* which means giving someone something he *doesn't* deserve. The difference between this and mercy is subtle, but important. When my wife has been mean to me, when she's been nasty or out of sorts, then she doesn't deserve for me to respond with kindness. So when I do respond kindly, I'm giving her what she doesn't deserve. That sort of response goes way beyond mercy. It's grace.

Love that forgives . . . love that is full of grace . . . is an essential for every—mark it—*every* marriage. No exclusions, no exceptions. That means *your* marriage. Why? Because husbands and wives are different by design and, on top of those differences, fallen and scarred by sin. As hard as we try, we can never fully fulfill the needs and expectations of our spouses. We will all, at times, stumble, mess up, fail. To paraphrase Scripture, "All of us sin and come short of the glory of God *and* the expectations of our spouses" (see Romans 3:23). But does this forgiving spirit shut down communication? Not at all. True love demands not only grace, but truth.

Love does not rejoice in unrighteousness but rejoices with the truth. So often today people try to get the upper hand through the careful practice of deception. They learn at an early age to disguise their feelings and create masks they can don at a moment's notice to maintain the image they desire. Lying becomes an easy, often accepted way of playing the game and winning. But in marriage, as in all of life, this win is in reality a loss. By God's scorecard, to be a winner one must first be a lover. And love never deals in deception; it traffics in truth.

This reality becomes clear with two definitions that help us come to grips with this aspect of love. Love that does not rejoice in unrighteousness means: *Love avoids sin.* And love that rejoices with the truth means: *Love joyfully partners with the truth.* It is obvious here that love has an emotional, motivational side to it. Love rejoices; it gets excited about certain things, and righteousness and truth are high on its list. Unrighteousness is not. Deception is not. Love tells the truth . . . no matter what!

We all want intimacy and joy in our relationships, and marriage is the most intimate human relationship of all. Honesty, though, is an essential prerequisite for real intimacy, and intimacy is an essential for real joy. Grace and truth are powerful allies in the battle for intimacy, joy, and romance. Without an atmosphere of grace and forgiveness, a husband or wife will not open up with the truth. And without the truth—honest disclosure of our dreams and expectations, failures and frustrations—the two will never really become one.

Love bears all things. To bear up under adverse circumstances for the welfare of others is real love, and it makes for a great definition for love that bears all things: *Love hangs tough.* When life throws unexpected or imperfect or irritating things our way, love can handle it. Love doesn't cut and run when problems crop up or start to pile up. To love like this means that we learn to do difficult things like tolerate imperfections, accept personal differences, and overlook selfishness.

Unfortunately, we Americans have, to a large extent, lost the ability to bear up under hardships. Unlike my parents' generation, we boomers and our kids have had it pretty easy. Yes, some have suffered, but most have grown up in a society committed to serving us the way we want it, when we want it, and how we want it. Just listen to the jingles of our generation: "You deserve a break today"; "Have it your way"; "We deliver for you." We want it *right,* and we want it *right now.* And if we don't get it our way, we won't come back.

As I write this chapter, believe it or not, I'm sitting in a local fast-food restaurant getting that "break" I deserve. I've noticed how frustrated, even angry, people get when they have to wait or when the order doesn't come out just right. As I look out the window at a sour-faced mother collecting her lunch at the drive-through, she reminds me of how spoiled we are.

The pioneers used to have to hunt for game, kill it, cook it, and then grind the wheat for bread just to have a good meal on the table. Many in the world today still face this drudgery—with joy. Our fast-paced, fast-food, quick-delivery culture is such a contrast.

I can remember the first time I bought a burger at a walk-up counter and didn't have to wait for it to be cooked. Wow! But then that seemed too slow. After all, I shouldn't have to get out of my car. Presto: the drive-in restaurant with carhops on roller skates delivering my tray of food and hanging it on the driver's side window. Then it got to where we were in too much of a hurry to even park, so drive-through windows began to appear. Just pull up, order, pay at the first window, and pick up your order at the next. Even this got to be too slow, and the lines became too long, and the lady in front of the guy in front of me was counting all that change. So now my favorite eatery has:

Step 1: A separate place for me to talk with a clown and place my order.
Step 2: A separate window for me to pause and pay as my food is being bagged.
Step 3. A window for slowing down just enough to grab my bag of goodies as I head for the door.

But today something seems to have gone terribly wrong. When this poor mother arrived at the pick-up window, her food wasn't quite ready. She had to wait maybe sixty seconds. A full minute, if you can imagine. The look on her face says it all to the sixteen-year-old kid at the window. "You idiots. Can't you get your act together? I want it right and I want it right *now!*"

The real problem, however, isn't that we want our food delivered that way. It's that we want *life* delivered right and right now. Husbands and wives want to have gourmet marriages delivered with drive-through efficiency and low cost. But just as great food can't be found at the drive-up window, so a great marriage doesn't come quickly for pocket change. It takes time to prepare a great meal, and it comes at a cost. Your marriage is no different. Are you willing to wait, to bear with one another? The feast will be worth it.

Love believes all things. Nothing builds up a loved one more quickly than a well-timed "I believe in you!" These are words with power, and when we wield them we slay the demons of defeatism. Conversely, nothing deflates more quickly than to cast doubt at the moment of commitment with a thoughtless question like, "Do you really think you can do that?" So our definition for a love that believes all things acknowledges this contrast. It says, *Love communicates confidence.* By communicating confidence, love gets into the construction business—the business of building up people. Love says, "I believe in you!"

In a very real sense, your husband or wife will likely become what you believe them to be. Your spouse is forever and profoundly affected by the messages he or she receives from you. Love encourages, believes in, pumps up the other member of the marriage flight crew. And why not, since the two have become one? You're in this thing together. Love one another by dreaming together and then chasing those dreams.

Love hopes all things. To hope means to expect or anticipate with pleasure and confidence. Hope knows where it's headed. It knows the outcome of the game before it even begins. It knows the final act before the curtain is raised. Hope may be based on God's promises for tomorrow, but love knows it's needed for today. Therefore, love looks for opportunities to deliver hope wherever and whenever it's needed. And it's needed all the time. Chuck Swindoll once said that hope is like electricity to a light bulb, water to a fish, or air to a jumbo jet. How true, especially in the context of marriage. A viable definition for love that hopes all things, then, is this: *Love is optimistic and smiles at the future.*

I've done a good bit of marital counseling, and I learned years ago that my first assignment as a healer is the resurrection of hope. Whenever I see hope restored, I know the couple has a chance of making it.

In the intimacy of marriage, our greatest fears and doubts spill out. My wife has heard my innermost thoughts and fears. It helps me just to talk about them with her. But one reason I let them out to my wife is that I can expect her to listen first, then love me with a good dose of hope-filled you-can-do-it I-believe-in-you stuff. And when she's down, I try to deliver the same prescription to her. In such a negative, pessimistic, you-can't-do-that world, we need injections of optimism from one another when we come home. It's been said that home is where the heart is. I would add that home is where the hope is. For anywhere we find hope, our heart will be drawn. Hope engages and energizes the heart of any husband or wife.

How do we communicate this kind of hope? Focus on the person and promises of God, and focus on progress, not perfection. You see, things don't have to be all roses for you to see some hope. You just have to quit focusing totally on the thorns. No matter how tough the times, how rough the relationship, where there is God, there is hope.

Love endures all things. This aspect of love refers specifically to tough times. Difficult circumstances. Love that endures all things means: *Love is willing to suffer.* A willingness to persist through pain, to suffer for another is no easy assignment. And why is it that we often struggle most in this area when it comes to the one we love the most? I think it's because husbands and wives give in too quickly to unrelated issues that convince them it's time to toss in the towel. Three come to mind: It's not *feasible,* it's not *fun,* and it's not *fair.* If I resist these distractions, though, and make up my mind to bear all things, believe all things, and hope all things, then the best way to express those convictions is to endure all things.

It may not seem feasible to love when you've been hurt, but it is worth the investment in your marriage. It may not be fun, but most things worth having will call you to endure a degree of pain before enjoying the delight of pleasure. And while it may not be fair, remember that marriages aren't built on "fair." They're built on love and grace. When I'm tempted to quit, I try to focus on the Cross. My Savior's love didn't quit on me. Doesn't my spouse deserve the same? Love doesn't quit.

Love never fails. This last phrase of 1 Corinthians 13 pulls it all together. Love never fails. Love never lets you down. It's always the path to take. Just do it! . . . and you won't be disappointed. So often husbands or wives think they have a better plan, a better blueprint, a new design for marriage. Don't try to outthink God, especially when it comes to love. God *is* love. He literally wrote the book on loving. Just do it—love His way—and it will never let you down.

GETTING STARTED

If you know anyone who works with words for a living, you've probably heard the term *writer's block,* the pesky phenomenon that can creep up on writers just as they sit down to begin working on a project or anytime between start and finish. The big question of how to start a story or sentence or paragraph can paralyze the most seasoned wordsmith and keep him or her from getting started or moving to the next step.

Practicing love in marriage can be like writer's block. Being unsure of where to begin or how to go about it, we stall, become frustrated, and fail to live out our own convictions. Just as most writers have ways of getting past the hurdles that stall their work, we're able to find in God's Word a number of key truths that are worth remembering as we begin this tender task of loving. They make a fitting conclusion to launch us on our adventure of loving.

Love is of God, not man, so get connected. It's evident in the New Testament letter of 1 John that commitment to loving God will have a ripple effect on all of life's relationships, including marriage.

Beloved, let us love one another, for love is from God; and everyone who loves is born of God and knows God. The one who does not love does not know God, for God is love. By this the love of God was manifested in us, that God has sent His only begotten Son into the world so that we might live through Him. In this is love, not that we loved God, but that He loved us and sent His Son to be the propitiation for our sins. Beloved, if God so loved us, we also ought to love one another. No one has seen God at any time; if we love one another, God abides in us, and His love is perfected in us. By this we know that we abide in Him and He in us, because He has given us His Spirit. (1 John 4:7–13)

From this passage we can make three significant observations, the three "R & P's" of love: Love is *rooted* in God's *person,* love is a *reflection* of God's *presence,* and love is a *result* of God's *power.* There are several implications to these observations.

The *first* is that apart from Christ I can never become the lover God wants me to be. Loving is not about trying harder; it's about trusting more deeply in Christ. When I trust and abide in Him, I rely on His power, not my own.

Second, loving is linked as much to who I am as to what I do.

The reason God is such a great Lover is that He is love. He wants to abide in us so that He can change who we are, a change that will be reflected in what we do. A view from the opposite perspective underscores this point. If love is reduced to simply what I do and not who I am, if I'm always trying to do something that I'm not, eventually I'll burn out. However, if what I'm doing is a reflection of what I'm becoming, it becomes more natural and, at times, even easy.

It's much more natural to be a loving servant-husband if God is remaking me on the inside into more of a loving servant-person. Then I can live out love in my marriage. I can do what comes naturally. The same is true of the wife seeking to love and respect her husband. As she grows in Christ, learning to love and respect Him, love and respect will flow into all her other relationships as well.

Finally, I need to focus on my spiritual life, which is the key to success in the rest of my life. When I'm growing spiritually, I become a more loving person even if I never study love the rest of my life. Why? Because the first fruit of the Spirit of God is love (see Galatians 5:22).

Haven't you ever wondered how Christian couples had great marriages before the avalanche of books on marriage hit the market? As much as I value my book on marriage and many that preceded it (and will follow), there is no substitute for the Spirit of God using the Word of God to make great husbands, wives, and marriages. One of my motivations for writing this book, quite frankly, is the observation that many volumes on marriage today virtually ignore the core passages of the Bible that we have addressed throughout these chapters. It is only as you walk with God that you will truly begin to walk with your spouse in joy and intimacy. Walk by the Spirit of God, with the Word of God as your guide, and you'll never be disappointed. However, trying to love in God's way without God's help is a recipe for frustration and failure.

If you've never received Christ as your personal Lord and Savior, do it now. Get connected so you can get started loving with His help, in His way, to His glory. May I suggest a prayer? If it expresses your heart, pray it now . . .

Lord Jesus, I need You. I need Your forgiveness and Your help if I ever hope to love my spouse the way I know You desire us to love.

I confess my sins and thank You for dying for me, for all my sins, on the cross. I believe in You, the resurrected Lord, and ask You to come into my life right now. Be my Savior and let me follow You as Lord the rest of my days. Thank You so much. I want to live and love for Your glory as long as I live. In Jesus' name. Amen.

If you prayed this prayer today, please drop me a line in care of the First Evangelical Free Church, 2801 North Brea Boulevard, Fullerton, California 92835, or E-mail me at dale@fefcful.org. I'd love to send you a gift to help you grow in the adventure of loving God's way.

Love is an act, not a feeling, so just do it. There comes a point when we need to realize that love cannot be linked to feelings, because that's not God's approach.

Little children, let us not love with word or with tongue, but in deed and truth. (1 John 3:18)

I'd paraphrase this as "loving with action and sincerity," which suggests that love is a behavior we choose. We live in a society that screams at us the misconception that love is something I feel, something I fall into, or something that captures me. One author said that "love is the feeling you get when you get a feeling you never felt before." Love generates feelings, but it is not at its core a feeling. At its core love is built on *character*, which we see reflected in our actions. It is reflected in how I choose to behave. When Jesus said I'm to love my enemies, for example, He translated love as an action, not a feeling. Nowhere in Scripture do I see God saying that when you run into your enemies, you ought to feel excited about seeing them. Jesus knows we don't have warm feelings toward people who mistreat us. So when He said, "Love your enemies," He was not talking about feelings; He was talking about *intentional behavior*. Love really is a choice. It's a choice I can make regardless of how I feel.

If love is being kind to someone who doesn't deserve it, if love is forgiving someone who doesn't deserve it, if love is passing up an opportunity to embarrass someone in front of other people when she (or he) does indeed deserve it, if love is treating someone far better than he or she deserves to be treated, then love is an action. It's choosing to do something even if emotionally I don't feel like doing it. If you're going to love your enemies, you have to do so in spite of your feelings.

Does this mean that love has nothing to do with feelings? No. But the Scriptures help us understand the proper relationship between feelings and love. Love *produces* feelings. Proverbs 5:18 tells a husband to "rejoice in the wife of your youth." Notice that it doesn't say, "Do right by the wife of your youth." And the next verse says, "Be exhilarated always with her love." The Hebrew word in this passage means to be intoxicated with her love. That's what I call an exhortation to let your feelings run deep. God loves feelings, romance, and all the joys of marriage. But those are not what we're to rely on as we love our spouse.

Love is a gift, not a wage or a bribe, so give it freely. Consider this passage from Luke's gospel.

> *"If you love those who love you, what credit is that to you? For even sinners love those who love them. If you do good to those who do good to you, what credit is that to you? For even sinners do the same. And if you lend to those from whom you expect to receive, what credit is that to you? Even sinners lend to sinners in order to receive back the same amount. But love your enemies, and do good, and lend, expecting nothing in return; and your reward will be great, and you will be sons of the Most High; for He Himself is kind to ungrateful and evil men. Be merciful, just as your Father is merciful.*
>
> *"Do not judge, and you will not be judged; and do not condemn, and you will not be condemned; pardon, and you will be pardoned. Give, and it will be given to you. They will pour into your lap a good measure—pressed down, shaken together, and running over. For by your standard of measure it will be measured to you in return."* (Luke 6:32–38)

While these verses are often used, and accurately so, to teach about financial giving, notice that their context is a discussion of the nature of love. They are not just a treatise on money. Jesus was saying that if we give love, we'll get love back. In fact, we'll get back even more than we give. That's a biblical principle and a promise. Notice also in verse 32 how Jesus' words fly in the face of our culture today: "If you love those who love you, what credit is that to you? For even sinners love those who love them." This is what I call love given as a *wage*. Conditional love. Love that says, "I'm loving you because you did something for me. My love is a payback." Isn't that how love is so often given today? Jesus said that's wrong. Love is to be a gift, not a wage.

Another abuse of love is to give it as a *bribe*. We see that in verse 34, which talks about love that expects something in return.

> *"If you lend to those from whom you expect to receive, what credit is that to you? Even sinners lend to sinners in order to receive back the same amount."* (Luke 6:34)

This is describing love given by a wife expecting her husband or kids to shape up. It's love given by a husband expecting his wife to reciprocate. Jesus said to give expecting nothing in return. Too often we give to prompt a payback. To do so is to love selfishly, which is an oxymoron if ever there was one. The irony is that if your love is a gift, freely given, you'll eventually get a return on your investment. But if the payback is your motive, you'll lose doubly. Both the joy of loving and the desired return will elude you.

Love is an obligation, not an option, so pay it. Romans 13:8 tells us to "owe nothing to anyone." This is another section of Scripture that's commonly used to teach a principle of financial management, with good reason. But notice again that the context provided by the rest of the verse reveals that its primary focus is something different.

> *Owe nothing to anyone except to love one another; for he who loves his neighbor has fulfilled the law.* (Romans 13:8)

Love is a debt, according to this text. It's the only legitimate debt we should carry. We should live with the attitude that love is not optional. It's *obligatory*. This is one debt we need to pay, freely, every time it comes due. The same idea is found later on in the New Testament.

> *Beloved, if God so loved us, we also ought to love one another.* (1 John 4:11)

That word *ought* is not a take-it-or-leave-it suggestion. It indicates an obligation to love one another in response to God's love for us. Understanding Christianity and understanding the uniqueness of God's grace should spur us to love. The message of Christianity is that God doesn't love us *because* we first loved Him. By grace He chose to love us *first*. And if the love of God has been showered upon me by grace, then logic suggests that I have an obligation to love other people, especially my spouse, by that same grace model. I would go so far as to say that it is immoral to hoard the love of God, which we did absolutely nothing to deserve. It's the gift designed to be given away.

Love must be grown, so nurture it. One of the marvelous mysteries of love is that it's dynamic. We can grow in love. We can also falter. At times we will even fail miserably. God's love never changes, but our capacity to love His way surely does. Oh, we may get good at it. Perhaps very good. Like the church at Thessalonica. When writing to them, the apostle Paul said he was "constantly bearing in mind your work of faith and labor of love," and that they had become "an example to all the believers in Macedonia and in Achaia" (1 Thessalonians 1:3, 7). When it came to loving, these folks had it down. But after praising their passion, listen to how Paul challenged them.

> *Now may our God and Father Himself and Jesus our Lord direct our way to you; and may the Lord cause you to increase and abound in love for one another, and for all people, just as we also do for you.* (1 Thessalonians 3:11–12)

Isn't that fascinating? Not only did Paul tell this group of exceptional Christians, who were known for their love life, to "increase and abound in love," but he also made it clear that a growing, maturing love was what he wanted in his own life and the lives of those closest to him. It's evident here that we who are intent on loving are in for a lifelong project. From the tenor of Paul's words, love is something we should never stop working on, especially when it comes to our marriages.

As if this weren't a high enough expectation, not many verses later we discover that the goal is not only to love more, to keep on growing in our capacity to love, but also to love better.

> *Now as to the love of the brethren, you have no need for anyone to write to you, for you yourselves are taught by God to love one another; for indeed you do practice it toward all the brethren who*

*are in all Macedonia. But we urge you, brethren, to **excel still more.*** (1 Thessalonians 4:9–10, emphasis added)

Read these verses again and let their message settle into your soul. Paul was writing to the one church in Asia that had a triple-A love rating. They were doing it well and "practicing" to get even better. And Paul was obviously pleased with their progress. His vision for the Thessalonians, though, and what he would hope for us as well, is that we and they "excel still more." Keep on growing in your love. Never stop. That was the desire of Paul's heart.

The question we must answer is, How do we make it the desire of our hearts? How do we abound still more? We take nothing for granted. We keep nurturing the most precious relationship called marriage. As taught in chapter 8, love is like a garden. If you want it to grow, you should tend to it regularly. Routine maintenance is a necessity.

Remember how we said just a few pages ago that love is neither a wage nor a bribe, but a gift, so give it freely? Look at this diagram:

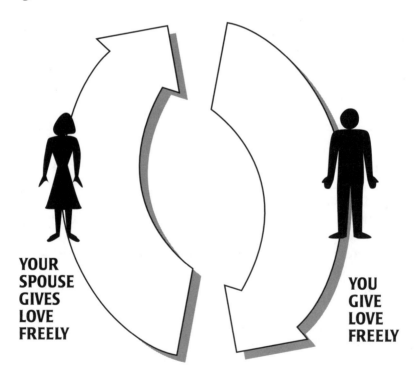

YOUR SPOUSE GIVES LOVE FREELY

YOU GIVE LOVE FREELY

Do you see the cyclical nature of a love relationship in which both husband and wife are committed to freely loving their spouse? It's like a perpetual motion machine. Each one's love, freely given, keeps the cycle going. If you choose to break the cycle—by withholding love or extorting love or abusing love—you both lose. However, when you want to get the ball rolling again, guess who has the ability to do so? *You both do.* So why not start now? Today. Those athletic footwear ads are right. "Just do it." And as you explore in God's Word the vast frontiers of love and how to express it to your wife or husband, be sure to follow Jesus' advice to His disciples. After telling them how to love God's way, He simply said, "Go and do likewise." God will bless you when you do.

IN CLOSING

Did God know what He was doing when He created us male and female? You bet He did! We are ever so different, but we are different by design. Men and women may indeed act like they are from distant planets. They may speak a different language. But the fact of the matter is, men are from Earth and women are from Earth—so let's deal with it and get on with life. Let's learn to view our differences as a gift from God, the creator of Mars, Venus, and every other planet in the universe.

God's Word contains detailed instructions for building a quality marriage. They are the blueprints for all of life and every relationship. Our Creator's plan incorporates and allows for all that is unique about us as men and women, husbands and wives. Just listen to His Word, and it will guide you step-by-step, day-by-day, hour-by-hour, as you build your marriage together. Like most great projects, it carries a high cost and won't be built in a day. But it will repay far more than you invest.

So no matter what the current state of your marriage, roll out God's blueprints, roll up your sleeves, and go to work! Build it strong, be creative, make it a thing of beauty, a home different by design.

Note: If this chapter on love has stretched your thinking and captured your interest, you may want to read the entire book from which it is based, *A Love That Never Fails,* also written by H. Dale Burke and published by Moody Press.

The Greatest of These is Love....

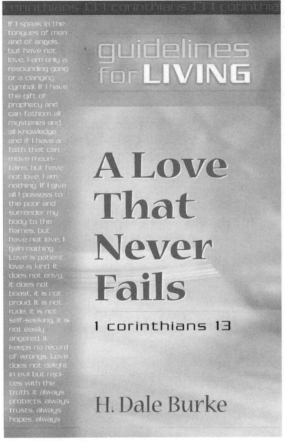

Guidelines for Living Series
A Love That Never Fails
1 Corinthians 13
H. Dale Burke

People seem to fall in love - and out of love - with everything from their cars to their mates. With the world's distorted view of love, it's no wonder Christians can't recognize godly love when they see it. God's love letter to us is 1 Corinthians 13, and it contains some of the most inspiring and practical teaching on love the world has ever known.

Paperback 0-8024-8798-1

MOODY
The Name You Can Trust
1-800-678-8812   www.MoodyPress.org

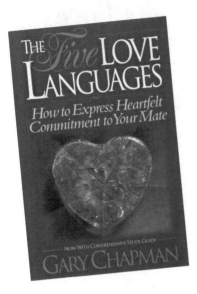

Learn to REALLY communicate love to your mate with the best-seller *The Five Love Languages.*

This bestselling book explores the all-important languages of love: Words of Affirmation, Quality Time, Receiving Gifts, Acts of Service, and Physical Touch. This book has helped millions of partners discover the best ways to communicate love and commitment to their mates.

OVER 1,000,000 IN PRINT.

Paperback 1-881273-15-6

Give the Gift of Love

Your Gift of Love
Selections From The Five Love Languages
Gary Chapman

What better gift to give a couple, new or seasoned, than an attractive book with excellent selections from one of the preeminent books on marriage to date? *Your Gift of Love* is a beautifully designed gift book containing key passages from Chapman's *The Five Love Languages*.

Paperback 1-881273-32-6

MOODY
The Name You Can Trust
1-800-678-8812 www.MoodyPress.org

Harness life's second greatest force.

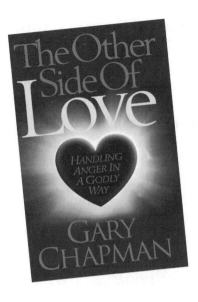

For many, handling anger is the single greatest challenge in marriage, family, and work. Best-selling author Gary Chapman teaches us how to handle our anger in a godly way. With practical guidance on making anger productive and learning to forgive, this book is a welcome response to common frustrations surrounding anger.

Paperback 1-881273-92-X

Love is the solution to your marriage struggles.

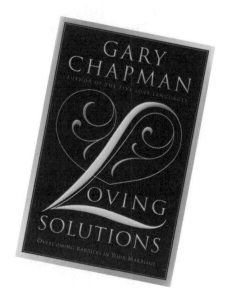

Are you living in a seriously flawed marriage? Gary Chapman offers hope. Discover practical and permanent solutions and take positive steps to change your marriage.

Gold Medallion Winner 1999.

Paperback 1-881273-91-1

MOODY
The Name You Can Trust
1-800-678-8812 www.MoodyPress.org

A New Kind of Small Group.

Marriage accountability groups provide the ideal environment for developing the marriages God intended. With a team of supporters at their side, every married couple can grow deeper and stronger in their love for one another. The book explains the groups and includes practical guidelines in forming and participating in one. The workbook walks couples through an actual group.

Paperback 0-8024-0946-6
Workbook 0-8024-0947-4

Revitalize Your Marriage in Just 12 Weeks!

Unlock time-tested secrets for building strong marriages with this insightful resource. With practical pointers on resolving conflict, cultivating intimacy, and much more, couples will be guided in building a marriage to last a lifetime. The workbook applies these principles and guides couples through a twelve-week study. Perfect for small groups!

Paperback 0-8024-3445-2
Workbook 0-8024-3446-0

MOODY
The Name You Can Trust
1-800-678-8812 www.MoodyPress.org

Moody Press, a ministry of Moody Bible Institute,
is designed for education, evangelization, and edification.
If we may assist you in knowing more about Christ
and the Christian life, please write us without obligation:
Moody Press, c/o MLM, Chicago, Illinois 60610.